So Maureen and John,

With happy memories of
one of the many evenings
when you have come to the
House yourself.

Greg Knight

10th November 1998

ABOUT THE HOUSE

Jill Knight by her London house in Lambeth, 1967.

ABOUT THE HOUSE

A Parliamentarian's Commentary

DAME JILL KNIGHT, DBE, MP

CHURCHILL PRESS
London

First published in 1995 by
Churchill Press Ltd
Number One, Wardrobe Place, London EC4V 5AH

British Library Cataloguing-in-Publication Data
Knight, Joan Christabel Jill
  About the House:
  A Parliamentarian's Commentary
  I.Title
  941.085092
  ISBN 0-902782-29-0

Designed by Heather and John Raybould
Set in 'Berthold' Melior
Typeset and printed by Goron Pro-Print Co. Ltd.,
Lancing, West Sussex, Great Britain

Contents

Foreword

The Right Honourable The Viscount Tonypandy PC, (Hon) DCL

WHEN Jill Knight first entered the House of Commons in 1966 she came as a breath of fresh air. In next to no time she was acknowledged to be a fearless and outspoken Conservative Back-Bencher.

People who make their mark in the House of Commons invariably enjoy friendships across all Party Political boundaries. Their loyalty to their own Party is in no way diminished by such friendships. Thus it was that the fiercely loyal Tory Jill Knight was held in high and affectionate esteem right across the Party Political spectrum.

Back-Bench MPs are the truest defenders of our Parliamentary Democracy, for they enjoy freedom to be critical of their own Party when they feel strongly on an issue which they believe is endangered. Jill Knight has never hesitated to speak clearly and without any ambiguity when her personal principles have been challenged.

Her courage revealed itself forcefully when the Commons first debated the issue of abortion. At that time it was almost unheard of for a woman to speak out as frankly as Jill Knight did. I well recall thinking 'She's a great fighter'.

In these Memoirs she tells her story with courteous candour. She has wielded great influence in the House of Commons, and has a fascinating account of her stewardship as MP for Edgbaston. Above all, she is a champion for the rights of children, and for the protection of family life.

This book, with its stories about life in the House of Commons, will also tell the reader much about the Author. I have long since believed that her moral courage springs from her firm Christian beliefs.

To read Dame Jill Knight's account of her thirty years in Parliament, is to be reinforced in faith in our democracy. She deserves the gratitude of our nation for the steadfast and upright way in which she has served us in the Mother of Parliaments.

GEORGE TONYPANDY
Speaker of the House of Commons
1976-1983

Acknowledgements

I am greatly indebted to Professor Donald Denman of Cambridge University for his help and encouragement in getting this book published and to my son, Andrew, who has done so much of the work of putting it together.

To them, and to the rest of my long-suffering family, I dedicate ABOUT THE HOUSE.

JILL KNIGHT

Picture Acknowledgements

The author and Churchill Press wish to thank the following individuals and organisations for their permission to reproduce their copyrighted photographs:

Birmingham Post & Mail (in Birmingham city centre 1966; campaigning in a vintage car 1966; fund-raising for a local charity; presenting school prizes; opening a block of flats for the elderly). Photographic Section, City Engineer's Department, Birmingham (tree-planting). Sport & General Press Agency (Conservative women MPs with the Rt Hon Edward Heath, PC, MP). *Glasgow Herald* (with Lord and Lady Home of the Hirsel). Srdja Djukanovic (Officers of the 1922 Committee of the Conservative Party with the Rt Hon Margaret Thatcher, PC, MP). The Press Association (Margaret Thatcher and Jill Knight). Three Star Press Agency (meeting the late King Faisal of Iraq). *L'Osservatore Romano Citta' del Vaticano* (An Audience with His Holiness Pope John Paul II). Monitor Press Features (Buckingham Palace, MBE Investiture, 1964). *The London Standard* (with the Rt Hon Selwyn Lloyd, PC, MP, 1960, and Buckingham Palace Investiture, 1985).

All the other photographs and items of ephemera are from the author's personal collection.

Front and back covers of the jacket: 'The Thames below Westminster' by Claude Monet, 1871, reproduced by courtesy of the Trustees, The National Gallery, London.

Preface

THIS book came to be written because hardly a week goes by without my receiving questionnaires and letters from students, researchers, pollsters and others who want to know what an MP's life is like. They display an insatiable curiosity about how one gets to be a Member of Parliament, what is one's motivation in standing for election, and how the British legislative system works. Perhaps what follows will answer at least some of the questions.

An old proverb runs: 'Take what you want, said God — and pay'. If you want the job of being a Member of Parliament, the true pay is in the currency of long hours, hard work, and a great deal of criticism.

The actual pay today in pounds sterling is a great deal better than when I entered Parliament 30 years ago. Even so, it is still well below the salary levels of MPs anywhere else in the Western world, and lower than in many other professions here at home; doctors, dentists, master chefs, top teachers, industrialists, many civil servants and a host of others earn far more. And when I began my Parliamentary career there was no pension at all — we frequently had to have a 'whip-round' amongst ourselves to help ex-MPs, some with very long service indeed, who had no money to live on. That problem, thankfully, has now been dealt with and a proper pension scheme introduced.

So much has changed during my time at Westminster. The workload has greatly increased, both in problems presented by constituents, and in Committee work. The former springs not from a more heavily beset electorate, but rather from the notion that a much greater range of subjects ought to be dealt with by their Parliamentary representatives; and from the near-universal belief that every single disaster befalling an individual can and should be officially rectified.

Thirty years ago, one would not even have *considered* approaching an MP because a shop had a leaky drainpipe which made the threshhold wet for customers; or because dogs fouled public land; or because one disapproved of a television programme. Today, such complaints as these appear regularly in the mail and at surgeries.

Respect was accorded MPs then, something which has greatly diminished today. Fuller and far more critical coverage of MPs' doings has brought that about. I do not think MPs of yore were any more moral, more clever or less culpable than they are in the 1990s. But the press acted differently. Every flaw and peccadillo was not highlighted, as it is nowadays, when immoral behaviour so gladdens the heart of the media.

Yet the job of being a Member of Parliament is still greatly desired — and no wonder, for the advantages are legion.

Time never, *never* hangs on your hands — every minute is spoken for, and boredom is unknown, save just possibly, occasionally, when listening to speeches.

You can choose almost any subject to study, be it prisons, education, hospitals or heritage; doors will quickly open for you, documentary material will become available, and you will find experts ready and eager to give freely of their knowledge.

Any MP who listens to his or her constituents will become wise in the ways of human nature. And those who study carefully the way Parliament works will be able to make their mark on legislation.

Best of all is the ability the job gives to cut through knots of intransigent bureaucracy, to help solve what are big problems for the people in one's small 'patch' — the constituency. Saving an old but charming group of houses from demolition, procuring an extra benefit for someone genuinely in need, helping carers or the disabled, getting constituents' points through to Ministers — all these things give real job satisfaction.

The girl I once was turns out to have been quite right, when she decided to seek to enter politics. Being a Member of Parliament is the most varied, the most lively and the most interesting job in the world.

September 1995   JILL KNIGHT

CHAPTER ONE

Ambition

I MADE up my mind to be an MP at the age of 13. This ambitious decision of mine was fired, in a contrary sort of way, by a keen and earnest Fabian schoolteacher who saw it as her duty in life to turn all her pupils into Socialists before they left her care. She taught me English, which, until her arrival, had been one of my favourite subjects. Actually it was more than that — it was a lifeline. Hopeless at Mathematics, I could always come top of English and History, and because my appalling Maths marks got lost in the average, school reports were at least passable.

The Fabian lady's guiding star was William Morris, who was rather old-fashioned even then, having held sway in late Victorian blue-stocking circles in the 1880s and '90s. He was a brilliant artist and designer who, detesting the industrial environment and class-ridden society of the late Victorian era, became one of the founders of Socialism.

She had us all studying his book *News from Nowhere*, which attempts to describe how England will be when the golden age of Socialism has dawned — that would be around the year 2000, according to the author's estimate. My teacher regarded this book as her bible. I thought it patently absurd, and the social structure described in it totally unworkable.

Morris describes a society in which no-one owns anything — not the house they live in, nor the clothes they stand up in. The State owns everything, but on the understanding that everyone can have anything they wish, just for the asking. There is a character in the book called the Golden Dustman. He gets his name from the gold lamé suit he always wears. He simply has a fancy for wearing gold lamé and enjoys wandering around thus arrayed. The suit is not his, of course, and never will be; some

1

sort of State store loaned it to him. He is quite happy with that — why would he need to own it? Whether such exotic raiment is suited to his calling, from a practical point of view, is never discussed. He wanted gold lamé, so gold lamé he has.

I read the book again recently, and what comes over to me now is the astonishing naïveté of William Morris's vision. He genuinely thought that abolishing wealth would automatically change human nature. All the people portrayed in his book as members of his new society are charming, good-tempered, hardworking, kind, hospitable and beautiful. The weather is always fine and people sing a lot. There are no crimes, no schools, no factories, no courts and no laws. No-one gets any votes because Parliament has been abolished. There is no marriage, no Monarchy and no God. And all this by the year 2000!

Each week we had to write an essay on two or three chapters of this book, and each week I fairly tore it to pieces. Mind you, I discovered rapidly that this was not the way to attain high marks. The more scornful I got in my compositions, the more irritated my teacher became. One day, when I had been particularly scathing, she wrote 'This is disgraceful work', in thick red pencil right across the page, and marked me one out of 10. I don't think I ever got more than three out of 10 for anything I wrote on *News from Nowhere*, and since I knew my grammar and syntax were not at fault, it was obvious that my opinions alone were causing my downfall. From having been top of the class in English, I was now bottom. My Maths marks being just as dreadful as ever, my average slumped heavily, and I got into a fearful row at home. But by then I had decided that if William Morris and my teacher were Socialist, I must be Conservative, and then and there I decided to go into Parliament.

Firm on this point — unswerving, even — I nonetheless kept my momentous ambition to myself for years: one casual mention of it to my scoffing brothers saw to that. Actually, I don't think I ever revealed it again until my husband proposed. I thought it only fair to tell him. Not that he believed me, of course, any more than my brothers had done years previously. It hardly looked likely to happen: I had no money, no useful connections, and no politics in the family. I had been born over a grocer's shop — which at the time didn't look a promising start.

Although my mother had gained a good degree at Bristol University, her marriage to my father had been a disaster; they divorced when I was five and I never saw him again.

I charted my course to Parliament with care. In spite of my parents' unsuccessful marriage, I made up my mind not to miss out on such an important part of life as husband and children. There was a lot to do. In 1947 I married a wonderful man who, once he realised how important a Parliamentary career was to me, always did everything to help, support and encourage me. Monty and I began married life as poor as church mice, but we were very happy.

As a member of the Young Conservatives in London before my marriage, I had helped to start several branches. Now I joined the YCs in my new home town, Northampton, and learned all about the joys of canvassing, the excitement of elections and the ever-necessary fund-raising efforts. I joined ward committees; I organised teams who would go along to Labour meetings and ask awkward questions; I attended Council meetings; I took volunteers to help in Parliamentary by-elections; I went to cheer the likes of Harold Macmillan, Rab Butler, Tony Barber and Quintin Hogg, whenever any of them spoke within a reasonable distance of my home. Monty and I even went to a rally addressed by Winston Churchill at Wembley. Old, lame and deaf though he was, he kept his huge audience enthralled; they adored him and cheered themselves hoarse.

Somehow, in between all this, my two sons, Andrew and Roger, arrived. We converted two top-floor rooms in our big Victorian house and let them for a peppercorn rent to a delightful girl who declared herself willing to baby-sit one night a week. Pam, incidentally, remains a dear friend to this day.

The post-war Attlee government was in power, and our

local Young Conservative branch was large in number and lively and enthusiastic in character. Every Christmas I wrote and produced a political pantomime for them — a project which increased membership and funds at about the same rate.

The first one was 'The House that Jack Built'. There was an acute housing shortage at that time. Bureaucracy ran riot. Regulations and restrictions covered every aspect of building houses, from the provision of bricks to the fitting of windows and doors or installing gas and electricity. The subject provided rich pickings for anyone looking to poke fun at the Labour Government. Problems for the pantomime's principal boy and girl in getting a roof over their heads were endless, until the magical Fairy True-Blue arrived, waved her Conservative wand and, in due course, everything worked out all right.

Another was 'Cinderella and the Three Bores'. The Bores were Fairy Staphyloma (Cripps), Fairy Clementina (Attlee) and Fairy Bevanda (Aneurin). I had masks made (early Spitting Image style) to resemble the political characters portrayed, and the three men taking the parts sported dark suits with red tape generously wound round them. They each had a charming little set of gossamer wings.

Another was entitled 'Little Boy Blue'. It featured 'Baron Promises', and a witch called Margarine Winterskill — an unkind jibe at Edith Summerskill, Parliamentary Secretary to the Minister of Food, who had lectured the nation that people should eat margarine rather than butter.

My pantomimes became quite famous in the area and we had large audiences. Meanwhile, I was asked to stand for the Local Council. Excellent! This was what I had aimed for, as it seemed the best way to learn my trade, while still being at home and looking after my family.

The political commitments fitted in well with the household routine. There was the main monthly Council Meeting, and my Committees (Education, Health, Children and what was then called the Watch Committee) met either at 10:00 in the morning, finishing in good time for me to get home to prepare lunch, or at 2:30 in the afternoon when the boys had gone back to school.

However, I have jumped the gun. I did not, of course, get on to the Council at the first try. Things are rarely that simple. As with Parliamentary seats, one was expected to fight what was deemed a 'hopeless' ward for two or three years before being offered something better when the chance came up.

Door-to-door canvassing became a way of life. This is a pastime which strikes terror into the heart of many a Conservative worker who has not had the chance to try it. In truth, canvassing is tremendous fun because of the endless variety attached to it, and the solid benefit it gives to a Candidate who has really tried. You may not win, but you learn a lot about people.

The first ward I fought (for about two years' running) was one which had never returned a Conservative Candidate and probably never would. The streets were mostly terraced houses near the town centre. I would start each night from the end of January and go on until May, when the Local Elections took place. Every night as soon as the boys were in bed and Monty had returned from work (about 6:30 p.m.) I would sally forth until 9:00 p.m., banging on the doors and trying to persuade people to vote for me.

It was not a good time of year for the operation, being dark and cold. Sometimes people would ask me in, and I always went, for fear of giving offence. When I look back now on the times I went into houses of which I had no knowledge, with people I had never met, I am amazed; but the violence which seems so much a part of today's scene was not so prevalent then, and it never entered my head that there could be danger. There were perhaps two or three times when I did wonder uneasily whether I had been wise to accept the invitation to 'come on in'.

One such case was when a huge man, who seemed to speak

very little English, responded to my introduction with a beckoning wave of his great hand. 'Kom', he said. In I went, quite merrily, thinking he was probably going to introduce me to his wife who would, of course, be English. Whether she was, whether she could speak it, or even whether she existed, I was never to discover. He led me into his front room, indicated a chair and ordered 'Sit!' — and disappeared.

What had he gone for? A wife? A mother? Or perhaps a knife or weapon? After a few minutes I stood up, apprehension growing, wondering if it wouldn't be best to tiptoe from the house. Luckily, just at that moment he came back, with a broad smile and a small book. It was a dictionary. Trying to translate my political spiel into Polish with its help was not a quick business. I left half an hour later feeling fairly confident I had succeeded, for his grin was broad when I assured him he was entitled to vote, and explained where my name would be on the voting paper.

In an even smaller street, not far away, I had a slightly different experience. The houses were mean and crowded, built around the turn of the century, with not a jot of architectural merit. You knew, before you crossed the threshold, that the front door opened onto a narrow passage. There would be a front room, and a back room, with a miniscule kitchen leading off. The steep stairs would lead to a couple of bedrooms. Probably there was no bathroom, and almost certainly the only lavatory in the place was outside the back door.

In answer to my knock the door opened about six inches. A wrinkled little face, with fly-away grey hair and piercing grey eyes appeared in the gap. Without waiting for any word from me, she roared abruptly, 'How do you spell rhubarb?'

I had done a fair bit of canvassing by then, but this reaction was one I had not heard.

I spelled the word out for her: 'R – H – U – B – A – R – B, I think', said I, but wondering what on earth was coming next.

'I wrote that down and it looks funny', she said doubtfully.

'It's a funny-looking word', I countered, which I think settled it.
Was she doing a crossword, planting a garden, or what? I
asked her. She cackled loudly. 'Me? A crossword? I couldn't see
the squares, let alone the print, me duck. It's me shopping list; I
reckoned I could do with a bit of loosening and I'll be down at
the market tomorrow.'

She asked me in after that, and we began a friendship which
lasted until the day she died. Rose was over 80, spry and sharp
as a tack, with a strong northern accent and a hilarious sense of
humour. She had an endless flood of stories about the time her
parents came down to Northampton from Teesside when she
was a small girl, after her two sisters had died of consumption
and when work was much easier to find in the Midlands. Her
memory was phenomenal. She had worked in a shoe factory
from 13 years of age and she could even describe the overall
and button boots she wore on her very first day, some 70 years
before. She was always one for the boys, she told me, with a
nudge and a chortle. One Christmas she'd jumped up on the
workbench and kicked her legs up so high that her pink garters
dazzled the whole shop and one of the 'Clickers'[1] fell in love
with her on the spot. They were soon married. Life must have
been very hard, but Rose chose only to remember what fun
they had — the works outings, the picnics in the summer, fairs
in Cow Meadow and paying twopence to squeeze into the gods
at the local theatre, to see the music-hall shows.

Her beloved Clicker was killed in the Great War, and they
had no children, so she was left all alone; but she never said
much about that. I used to go and see her whenever I could,
and she never failed to make me glad I had taken the time to
visit. Sometimes I took my children, to her great delight. Even
when she lay dying, tiny and clean in a hospital bed, she could
still manage her infectious chuckle, and she said quite
outrageous things to try and shock the rather stern and

---

[1] Clicker: a man who cut leather with a curved knife, working round small
brass-bound patterns which clicked rhythmically as he discarded them. A
craftsman at his job.

unbending Ward Sister. She told me with a broad wink that she quite fancied the young Houseman, and indeed I once saw her positively bat her eyelids at him.

Sir Walter Clegg, for some 21 years the Member of Parliament for South Fylde in Lancashire, was one of the friends and colleagues with whom it was a joy to swap canvassing stories. He told me he once fought Ince — not a seat I know, but I understand it was in an industrial town in Lancashire. In the whole of the cobbled streets of Ince, Walter assured me, there was hardly one Conservative. And as he trudged up the roads knocking on the doors for support, he frequently got them slammed in his face, while his ears rang with some highly uncomplimentary phrases.

Those houses must have been even smaller than the ones I had been canvassing, for Walter said that the front door would open straight into the front room. Towards the end of an evening of door-slamming and verbal abuse, he finally thought he had struck oil when one woman opened the door wide enough for him to peep in and see there, hanging on the opposite wall, a large framed picture of Benjamin Disraeli.

'At last', he thought, 'a friendly reception.' He summoned up an extra-ingratiating smile and after a quick glance at the canvass card, to be sure of getting her name right, began: 'Mrs Kelly? I'm so pleased to meet you and I have a feeling that you'll be pleased to meet me too, because I see that picture of Disraeli, that wonderful old Conservative leader, on your wall. My name is Walter Clegg, and I am the Conservative candidate in this election!' Her eyes blazed. 'Disraeli nothing!' she screamed. 'Sure 'tis my cousin Seamus who was killed in the Easter Risin' an' if you're a Tory you can get the hell outa here!'

It was probably about that time that Walter decided he couldn't win — in Ince, anyway — but it didn't take him long to win elsewhere, and from then on Ince's loss was South Fylde's gain.

Canvassing teaches more about people than any other exercise. You never know what you will find behind the doors you knock on. It could be one of the bustling, cheerful souls, who will offer you a cup of tea. It might be one of the taciturn ones, the voluble ones, the dull or the totally uninterested ones. It could be one of the retired professional people with lots of time who will waste yours shamefully, given half a chance. Not wasted *intentionally*, but simply because he or she has lots of theories, and too few opportunities to talk about them. One must learn to distinguish between these and the ones who *do* try to waste your time on purpose — political opponents who know you won't be furthering your cause while on their doorstep, and who will deliberately aim to keep you talking to stop you canvassing. Any Party worker worth his salt can spot 'em a mile off.

It never fails to amaze me, the things people will tell total strangers. Extra-marital affairs, the dubious parentage of various relatives, even their own deepest feelings roll out in an endless tide, if the face is too sympathetic and the ear too ready. I remember one woman, who confided that she had just realised that her whole marriage had been soured by the presence of relatives: 'All my married life', she said, 'the whole lot — nearly forty years — we've either had his mother or my father living with us. We've never, ever, been alone. It's just struck me that our marriage never really stood much of a chance, and now it's too late, of course.'

An Agony Aunt I am not, and there seemed little I could say to help her. But she was marking a change in English social history. Years ago, when my parents were young, it was the norm to have Granny or Grandpa permanently in the place near the fire. Many today deeply regret the change, and certainly I find it sad that families are more fragmented than they used to be, but I can quite see that woman's point of view, and understand her bitterness. Alas, not all elderly people are gentle little lavender ladies, or bluff, kind old gentlemen.

CHAPTER TWO
Apprentice Years

THERE have been many changes in the attitudes of voters, since those early days when I began canvassing. There has, too, been a shift in the way canvassers themselves think about the areas they canvass.

At one time Council housing estates could be guaranteed to return a rock-solid Labour majority whenever called upon to vote. Not so today. Since 1987, when the blue-collar vote went Conservative, and the plushier areas, contrariwise, grew wobbly in their support for the Tories, it has no longer been possible to give an accurate assessment of political intention by looking at the house a voter lives in, or the character of his neighbourhood.

When Herbert Morrison sought to enlarge the Labour vote in certain London constituencies by building Council flats there, he was on to a winner. Conservative councillors alleged to have tried similar tactics to increase their vote in Westminster, 40 years later, were on infinitely more uncertain ground; they were much more vilified, with far less cause, since things are just not that simple any more.

The volatility of today's electorate poses far more of a challenge to the party campaigner. Voters know much more about what is going on. Politicians are subjected to questioning — often quite mercilessly — on TV and radio. Newspaper reporters blatantly ignore the old honourable 'off the record' conventions, and use every trick in the book to get a story — too often inaccurate, many times compiled of half-truths. The public is not always *well*-informed — but it is certainly informed! Opinion moves and changes with fashion quite as much as clothing, furniture or architecture, and the strongly-held opinion of a minority changes the actions of the majority. It

11

would be unthinkable today to have a canvassing experience like this one of mine in the 1960s ...

She was a gentle and friendly lady. She lived not a hundred yards from a shoe factory — the factory where her husband had worked all his life. We spent half an hour talking Conservative policy, and she agreed with everything I said; so when we were done, I dared to express the hope that her vote would be cast my way. 'Well', she said, 'you seem a nice young lady, and all you say is quite right. But ... my husband was a Labour man all his life and I always vote Labour. In his memory, you understand.' Enough to make a feminist weep!

On another dark and cold night in those early days, I knocked on a rather dingy door, and heard slow and heavy steps coming along the passage, which clearly boasted no carpet. A bolt was withdrawn (laboriously) at the top; another at the bottom. A key rasped in a lock, and finally the door opened a good six inches, held in check by a stout chain.

A voice snapped: 'What do you want?' I shifted closer to the gap and explained that I had come about the Council elections. The door closed, the chain was withdrawn, and a crack appeared in Fort Knox.

'You'd better come in', said the voice. Shutting the door behind me, I followed a strange shape down the passage. He was outlined against the light at the end, and I could see that he had his trousers rolled up over his knees. We entered the kitchen. It was dominated by a huge black range on one side, and a deal dresser, crammed with china, on the other.

My host sat down and plunged his feet into a large galvanised-iron bowl, half-filled with steaming water. Friday night was clearly his night for washing his feet.

'Get on with it then', he said. I stared fixedly at the range (anything to avoid looking at his knees) and began talking about the need for wise and careful management in Local Government.

'Do you mind passing over the kettle?' he said, 'I likes it a bit 'otter than this'. I gingerly picked up the enormous blackened kettle, carefully using the bit of sacking perched on the large handle. It weighed a ton. Very cautiously I poured some hot water into his ablutions, trying to avoid any splashing. I staggered back to the range with the kettle. He grunted.

I went on with my sales talk, with a couple of small interruptions — passing him first a towel, then some rather evil-looking powder with which he proceeded to dust his nice clean feet.

'All right then, I'll think about it', he said. 'But you'd better get out of here because my wife will be back any minute, and if she sees you here, with me like this, *she* won't vote for you.' Time, as they say nowadays, for a sharp exit.

All this was grist to the mill of my experience; but I knew I had to do a darned sight more than canvass, if I were ever to get where I wanted. There were very, very few women in Parliament, and the proportion of constituencies which would choose a woman to fight a winnable seat remained obstinately low. Somehow I had to become widely known in the Party nationally — and I had to learn to speak confidently in public, too.

I accepted every request to speak that came my way. Big meetings or small ones; political or non-political gatherings; church groups, Townswomen's Guilds, Ward suppers, debating societies — all were opportunities for me, and I took them on eagerly.

Monty, a lot of kind friends and Pam did noble service in having the boys for me, though there were a few occasions when I could take them with me.

One such was when I was asked to open a church bazaar in a village some miles outside Northampton. It was to be held in the vicarage garden or, said the posters, 'In the village hall if wet'. As is woefully common on these occasions, the day dawned with the rain coming down in stair-rods from a leaden, unrelenting sky. The hall was crammed. Stalls were jammed in, proffering splendid collections of cakes, pickles, tea-cosies, bed-socks, white elephants, jumble, tombola, and dear knows what all. Scores of would-be purchasers packed all available space and a small group of clergy, bolstered by the presence of no less a personage than the rural dean, were to be seen at the back. The obligatory tot in frilled organdie clutching a large bouquet for the opener was held in check at the side of the tiny stage.

The boys sat, transfixed. I had intended to end my short speech with the thrilling words: 'and now I have pleasure in declaring the bazaar open'. To my utter horror I *heard* myself say: 'and now I have pleasure in declaring the bar open'.

I waited for raised eyebrows and disapproving stares. Especially from the dean. Instead, a sea of pleasant faces smiled back at me, and hands clapped in approval. The bouquet was presented without a hitch. I learned the interesting lesson that people don't hear what you *say*; they hear what they *think you are going to say*. I knew what I had said, and I felt myself going scarlet to the roots of my hair because of it; but not another soul noticed.

There are many techniques one needs to master if one is going to be a good public speaker. Avoid mumbling, losing your drift, going on too long, or swaying from side to side. Check your appearance. I once sat through a speech by a man whose flies were undone. I'm sure the audience *tried* not to stare fixedly at the aperture, but I don't think they heard a word he said.

Avoid speaking with an uncurtained window behind you — it is exceedingly trying for an audience to have to look at a speaker against light. If the audience is fairly small, don't speak from a high stage — commandeer a couple of spare men and get them to bring the Chairman's table down to ground level. (Er, better ask the Chairman first.)

Ideally, one's voice must be clear and it must carry. You can be giving the most magnificent and riveting peroration since Mark Anthony: if the audience can't hear you, you may as well be reciting a laundry list. Earlier I had done some training as a singer, so I did know how to make my voice carry, and this has helped me a lot in my political career.

It also occurred to me that one held the attention of one's audience far better if there were highs and lows; funny bits as

well as serious ones. A touch of drama helped. And for
goodness' sake never go on too long. That can't be said too
often!

The speaking invitations started to increase, and after I had
gained a standing ovation for a speech at a Conservative Party
Conference, requests for my services flooded in. All these
opportunities gave me invaluable experience, and all of them
helped to make me better known in the Party too, which was
very important if I were to gain a seat. Some of them provided
hilarious experiences, and some, when I actually started out, I
regretted ever making. Such a one occurred on a night in the
depths of winter. The meeting was in the Dukeries, in
Leicestershire. There was thick snow, icy roads and patchy fog.
The meeting was timed for 8 p.m. and I was invited to the home
of the Constituency President for dinner beforehand.

Having got my boys to bed, and with Pam on babysitting
duty, I picked up my notes, pointed my small car north and set
off. The directions had said that I should find some lodge gates,
after which there was a drive of about a mile up to the house.
The drive was single-track, and not in good repair. The snow
coated numerous potholes. Sometimes my headlights picked
out small trees on the slopes at the side and once a hare darted
across in front of me. I crawled along in the dark countryside —
definitely low-gear terrain — and finally, just as I had decided I
must have been going for about two miles, the track curved
around and I made out the outline of a very large house ahead.
It was built like Buckingham Palace, in a hollow square. I drove
through a high stone gateway and found the front door. It was
iron-studded and about five feet wide. There was a bell-pull. I
tugged it energetically.

After about three minutes I heard it clang dolefully,
somewhere deep inside. Another long wait. Finally I heard slow
steps shuffle, like something out of a Hammer House of Horror
movie. The illusion did not go away. The huge door opened

slowly with a spine-tingling creak. The oldest butler in the world stood revealed.

'Mi . . . i . s . iss Knight?' he quavered. 'The Co . . . lo . . . nel is ex . . . pec . . . ting you.' He turned with stupendous dignity and set off at a pace which would not have taxed a tortoise suffering from bunions. I followed. The trek took some time but finally, past sets of armour, ancient mirrors, portraits and monumental pieces of furniture, we reached a door which the old boy didn't so much throw open as persuade ajar. I was announced to my host and given a glass of execrable sherry.

The Colonel and his wife took me to the dining room, which was in true baronial style: crossed swords; shields and tapestries adorned the walls. My host was seated at one end of a long table, my hostess at the other end and I was placed exactly equidistant from the two — roughly 10 feet away from each. I don't remember what we ate for the main course. The meal was served by the Ancient (I never saw any other member of staff) and was stone-cold by the time it reached us. The pudding I shall never forget. Methuselah doddered towards me with a huge silver entrée dish, placed it on the table beside me and removed the large and impressive cover which was fetchingly engraved with a complicated coat of arms. Nestling in the middle of a dish at least two feet long were three small banana fritters.

I don't know whether it was the fritters or something previously eaten in the course of this odd meal, but I began to have violent indigestion and with mounting horror contemplated the meeting which was to come. I was not sure my voice would be loud enough to drown the noise my indigestion was causing. I asked if I might go to the bathroom before we left, for surely there *must* be a bathroom-cupboard in a bathroom, and surely inside it *somewhere* there would be some Rennies, BiSoDol, or other useful chemist's remedy for my problem.

The bathroom, like everything else in the house, was enormous. It was painted a virulent shade of green. An Edwardian bath on claw-and-ball feet was to be seen cowering in one corner but — oh joy! — there *was* a bathroom-cupboard. I rushed across and flung it open. It was Mother Hubbard empty, save for one dead moth. I have never travelled since then without some indigestion tablets in my handbag.

On another occasion I was to speak to what was known as a 'Tory Tea Club'. These occasions were usually held in village halls. A tea was provided by the Committee and other volunteers. Card tables were set out with delightfully hand-embroidered table-cloths, and each table had a tasteful vase of flowers set in the middle. Four people sat at each table. After enjoying a tea which was infinitely better than that dinner in the Dukeries, the audience then prepared to listen to the speaker. I fancy that for them the tea was, as it were, the sugar, and my speech was the pill. I hope I was good for them.

Opposite each other at one of the tables at this Tory Tea sat two friends — one a lady Committee member, I believe. Next to the other sat a little old lady wearing a hat with a good deal of dotted veiling around the brim. Having had tea, one of the two friends brought out a packet of cigarettes. The other fumbled for her lighter, then reached across the table, to light her friend's cigarette. Just at that moment there was an unfortunate breeze. A spark appeared in the depths of the veiling on the old lady's hat. She did not notice this, since she had her head turned away towards the platform, and was listening avidly to the Chairman introducing me. I, of course, could see everything, but do nothing. I watched the spark on the hat grow to a small flame; the two friends, guilty but politely silent, took steps to end the conflagration. One picked up her gloves and dealt the flame several large blows, but it continued to burn away merrily. So the other, with great presence of mind, seized the flowers out of the vase and emptied the water on to the hat, still on the head of its thunderstruck owner.

She gave a strangled cry of sheer terror and scuttled out of the room. She had no idea that her hat was on fire and because the Chairman was speaking, nobody liked to make a fuss. I don't suppose they saw her at any Conservative meeting ever again and I can only imagine what she probably said to her

friends: 'My dear, don't you go anywhere *near* those
Conservatives! There was I, last Tuesday, sitting quietly
listening to the Chairman, when one of those women started
hitting me quite hard on the head with her gloves, and then the
other one poured a whole vase of water all over me. I think
they must be mad!' She probably joined the Labour Party the
following week.

Later on, when my sons were a bit bigger, I did sometimes go
away overnight, and on one occasion I was speaking at a
meeting in Wales. It was arranged that I should stay with the
Conservative President and his wife, who actually lived in a
castle. A very impressive place it was, too. There was a
splendid hall with a staircase going up from the middle and
then branching out to the east wing on the left and the west
wing on the right — just the sort of thing that would have
appealed to Topol in 'Fiddler on the Roof'. My hostess took me
upstairs to show me my room, which was some quarter of a
mile down at the end of a very long and wide corridor. We
passed suits of armour, large brass-bound chests, mysterious
cupboards and sets of antlers on the walls. My room was
roughly the size of a tennis court and had a bathroom leading
off it. There were two beds; my hostess indicated the one which
had been made up for me. I noted with some apprehension the
candles and matches on the bedside table. Always beware of
such adjuncts. They indicate a sure-fire certainty that the
electrical supply is unreliable.

Late that night, after the meeting and a nightcap with the
family, my hostess showed me again to my room and bade me
goodnight. I took a bath and then trotted over to the bed I was
supposed to sleep in. Throwing back the covers I discovered a
miniature lake in the bed. It didn't help that the mattress was
rather old and had a deep valley in the middle. Water lapped
around the sides. An empty stone hot-water bottle lay half-
submerged. I considered the possibility of trying to lie only on the

uplands, curled round the sides of the lake, but realised this would be hopeless — I would be bound to slide in the night. Clearly someone would have to be found. I went to the door and opened it: pitch blackness. I had no idea where the light switches were and I went back to find the candle and matches from my bedside table. I lit the candle and started to grope my way down the corridor. It was a terrifying experience. The candle flickered and I was afraid it would go out. 'Help!', I called out. 'Is anyone there?' Seemingly not. I tried again — 'Hello!' I yelled. But not a soul answered. The whole place was black and silent, and very eerie. When my pathetic little candle flame finally died on me, I realised that there was nothing for it but to go back. The other bed in the room was about 20 feet away over near the window. It was not made up and the blankets were damp. There was no alternative: I had to sleep in it.

The lesson I learned from *that* was not so much to take a dry blanket on my travels but to make sure I knew where my hostess slept, and to examine my bed before she was out of earshot.

Things have changed a lot in the Conservative Party since then. Our Presidents hardly ever live in castles, or mini-Buckingham Palaces — semis or Council flats more likely. Few women wear hats (once *de rigueur*) at lunches or Conferences. Whether such changes are positive I would not like to say, but there is no doubt that changes were needed in the attitude of some of the Conservative ladies. I like to think I made my tiny contribution to this.

It happened that I was due to speak at a Conservative Ladies Luncheon at a large hotel in the North Midlands. This function was to take place in the ballroom — a very grand affair with many Grinling Gibbons-type swags of fruit and flowers on domed ceiling and pillared walls, and much cream, gold and green paint around. The ballroom was on the second floor. Coming out of the lift, one walked along a very wide corridor, and there, at the entrance to the ballroom, sat a very grand lady at a very small card table, which was covered with bits of paper and money. As I approached, the Duchess (surely she could rank no less?) raised scornful eyes to me, extended a plump white and be-ringed hand and said, 'Tickahte?'

'I am so sorry I am afraid I don't have a ticket', I faltered. Her Grace's eyebrows rose. There was a pause. 'You don't have a tickahte?' she said witheringly. 'Er ... er ... no. I'm afraid not. Sorry.'

She looked me up and down. 'Well, are you with sombodeh?' she grated.

'No, I'm afraid I am quite alone.'

Her Grace frowned majestically. It was not a pretty sight. 'You can't come in heah.' I tried to blush. I increased what I hoped was not too theatrical a display of dithering apology.

'Oh, I'm *so* sorry. I b-beg your pardon.' I turned my back and started to walk out, and I had every intention of doing so. Then the staggering thought struck her. This insignificant little person surely but *surely* could not possibly be the speaker ... could she ... could she?

'Just a moment', she called imperiously after my retreating back, by now nearly at the last potted palm. 'You are not the speakah, are you?' I stopped in my tracks, I turned. A charming smile lit up my features. 'Do you know, I really believe I was to have been', I said.

She jumped to her feet. Her bosom caught the edge of the table which tipped over, scattering tickets, money and envelopes all over the place. I had the satisfaction of noting that the Duchess's face was bright puce. Her apologies were abject as she passed me on to a member of the Committee. I would hope and trust that she never treated a possible young recruit to the Conservative Party in that way again.

CHAPTER THREE

Credentials of a Councillor

JUST after the May local government elections in Northampton in 1956, when I was again beaten in St Crispin Ward, a senior Conservative Councillor died. I was invited to fight the by-election, which was to take place on June 28th. There was the usual concern as to whether we could get the electors out to vote, only about six weeks after they had trooped out for the last lot of elections, but we all threw ourselves enthusiastically into the fray, with the other side doing the same. The situation was fraught for both sides because so long as I held onto the seat, the Conservatives would have equal representation with Labour, and if they won, control of the Council would pass into their hands.

As the local paper put it, reporting on the by-election on June 29th, 'Mrs Jill Knight romped home with a drop of only 22 votes on last month's majority'. I had successfully negotiated the first step. I knew only too well how far there was still to go, but I was on my way. Monty and I had a small celebration that night.

In those days things were very different on local Councils. For a start, no-one was paid any money — one gave one's time and service quite freely. Public-spirited employers allowed time off for their employees to do Council work and self-employed businessmen were able to claim a small amount of money to cover their absence, when often they would have lost orders or been unable to complete contracts whilst doing Council work. But there was no *pay* in the way there is today.

It is doubtful whether paying allowances to Councillors has improved the quality of those offering themselves for service and it is highly questionable whether the ratepayers have benefited, because paying Councillors has pushed up the cost of Local Government tremendously.

21

The job was never intended to be, and should never have been allowed to become, a full-time one anyway. In every Council headquarters there are suites of offices crammed with full-time well-paid officials, there to do the Council's bidding and to work out all the implications of schemes under consideration by Councillors. They are trained and capable to do the sums, tabulate advantages and disadvantages, allocate housing points, road repairs or library services, and all the minutiae of running Councils to a master plan laid down by the democratically elected local representatives. There should be no need for a second tier of paid public servants in the town halls.

Since the demise of the voluntary, unpaid Councillor, the numbers of meetings have increased greatly — and it surely cannot be denied that one powerful reason for that increase is that the more meetings the Councillors attend, the more money they usually get. Council business can always be made to extend to fill the time made available for it.

Even when the scheme started, there were dissenting voices, and two of the best Councillors I have ever known resigned when the payment started, saying that there should be ways to give one's time and efforts for one's town or city, without expecting payment.

The first thing I learned as a member of the Northampton County Borough Council was that I should spend ratepayers' money 10 times more carefully than I would spend my own. This advice was wise and right; I only wish that it was dinned into today's Councillors as thoroughly as it was into us.

There were very few women on the Council, and those who *were* there tended to be fairly elderly or unmarried. I was the only one with young children and everything I did had to be slotted in with the job of running the house, cooking the meals, doing the shopping and so forth. Monday was my washday and it was also the day of the week when the Council met — not every week, of course, but on the last Monday in the month the full Council assembled and passed (or argued over) all Committee reports presented during the preceding four weeks.

Council Meetings would often go on for hours. I remember sitting in the Council Chamber at about 9:00 p.m. one night, when it struck me, as I looked around, that no other Councillor had all the ironing to do when he got home. My male colleagues, undoubtedly exhausted after a long day at work and then having been in Council for two or three hours, would be greeted at home by a sympathetic wife: 'Sit down and put your feet up, dear, the meal will be ready very shortly.' When I got home, on the other hand, three pairs of eyes would look up at me and ask when supper was going to be ready. I would dash off my hat, reach for my apron and head for the stove — and perhaps the ironing board afterwards, stomachs being duly filled.

❄

Today one of the hazards for women MPs is that hundreds of questionnaires come in regularly from an enormous number of sources — the senders announcing, as if they were attempting something that had never been done before, that they are conducting a survey as to why so few women are in Parliament. When I began my bid for Westminster it had a lot to do with the need to be utterly single-minded and prepared to give up all the recreations which one's friends enjoyed. I had time for running the house, looking after my family, and politics — nothing else at all.

This certainly does not mean that most women are frivolous creatures who prefer to chase fun rather than advancement, but when one is young, one has to be very serious indeed about a political career to give up everything else in the hope of attaining it. Perhaps I had a special advantage in that I very much enjoyed the business of bringing up my children, reading to them, teaching them things and watching them develop. I think one of the saddest remarks I have ever heard was from a Women's Lib supporter who announced grimly on television that, for a woman, having a child meant 15 years' hard labour.

I enjoyed most of the Council work, too, and learned a lot. How a town is run, for instance; what happens in an epidemic; how an old persons' home should be organised; where street lights should be placed; when children should be taken into care; what services are most needed by the blind, the disabled or the mentally handicapped – and a host of other lessons which have stood me in good stead ever since.

Council officials were almost invariably expert, courteous and helpful. The natural attitude of a Councillor or MP is to side with constituents against officials. I learned that it is wise to get the official's side before making any judgement at all, though judgement may well come down on the side of the individual in the end.

More than one Council matter gave me sleepless nights. There was the family whose tiny baby had been taken into hospital twice – once at the age of one month and again at two-and-a-half months. Each time the child was found to have open safety-pins in his stomach. On the *third* occasion the doctors at the hospital notified the Children's Department, saying that they could not operate again on a such tiny child (by then he was about six months old) and that he would die if such a thing happened again. The Children's Officer advised the Committee to take urgent legal action to have the child discharged from hospital into Council care, to avoid his being returned to his parents.

The parents contested the action. To our utter amazement the magistrates supported the parents and said that the child must be discharged to them. How on earth any of them thought a baby under six months could crawl around picking up and eating open safety pins we did not understand, but although the strongest possible representation was made on behalf of the Committee in the Court, it was no use.

Two months later the child was dead from obstructions in its stomach. X-rays revealed open safety-pins.

Although there are certainly some bad parents, it always comforts me to realise that the overwhelming majority are good and caring. I recall being asked to go and see one family in their home. I found a little lady, well over pensionable age, intelligent and active. With her was her son. Obviously badly mentally handicapped, he must have been about 42, although she told me he had a mental age of five. Ever since his birth his mother had looked after him. She never had a holiday. She had never left the house without him. On every shopping trip, every errand, Tommy had to accompany her, for he could not be left in the house by himself. By the time her husband retired and could have helped, Tommy was so used to going out with her that he would scream unceasingly if she left the house without him.

She had fed him, washed him and cared for his every need for 42 years. As I listened to her I tried to picture what her life must have been like. I couldn't really do it.

But her object in asking me to call was not to complain and certainly not to make a catalogue of her care for him. Her simple point was that she was worried about what would happen to Tommy when she died.

This is still a problem for many parents of such 'children'. There is an answer, with the provision of more hospital places for the badly mentally handicapped, to the basic question of keeping them warm, fed, washed and clothed. But no institution can ever compare with the kind of care that Tommy had received from his mother. The extent to which a poor clouded mind must suffer, when that care is finally withdrawn, is appalling to contemplate.

Modern studies and trained and experienced doctors in the field have advised that many of the less badly afflicted are far better out of institutions than in them, and indeed in my Council days I used to question in my mind why some mild and harmless inmate should have been locked up for 30 years or more. But for such a policy to work there must be back-up community care, constant help and guidance, and assured accommodation. Much of this was woefully lacking when the changes first came about, though it is better now.

In Tommy's day very little indeed was done for the mentally handicapped save locking them away, and it was not a

fashionable cause. Many parents seemed, tragically and un-
necessarily, to feel a burden of shame at having had a mentally
handicapped child in the first place, and some still do. Almost
all of them shoulder the most incredible burdens un-
complainingly, and deserve every possible support and understanding, which the public do not always show. There was one
Centre for mentally handicapped children in Northampton
where the mothers would take them in the morning and fetch
them back in the afternoon. Having visited that Centre one day,
I came out at the same time as the children did and was
shocked to see mothers with ordinary children passing by, who
pulled their child away to avoid contact with the little mentally
handicapped ones. Yet any family in the land can have such a
child — there is no virtue involved in having a normal one, only
luck.

Every Councillor was expected to take a certain allocation of
outside work, of trusteeships, governorships and memberships
of various charitable bodies. I was assigned to the Association
for the Blind, who had a splendid workshop which produced a
wide range of goods, and many things were done for the blind
in the way of special housing and other facilities. There was no
shortage whatsoever of people willing to take up Board places
for this truly excellent cause. But quite the reverse situation
obtained where mentally handicapped persons were concerned, so I asked if I might change over and direct some of my
activities to that field.

Later I became Chairman of the Board of a school for
educationally sub-normal children. It was housed in one of the
oldest school buildings in the town and conditions were almost
Dickensian. I found that frequent applications for a new
building had been turned down in favour of other schools for
normal children and no-one seemed to care that these children,
already badly handicapped by nature, should also be handicapped by being taught in the worst school buildings of all. I

took up the cudgels, and, after quite a lot of campaigning, led a small delegation to see the then Minister of Education — Sir Edward Boyle. We got our school.

In some ways, work as a Councillor can provide greater immediate satisfaction than work as an MP. There are tangible products, like that school, from which one gets deep satisfaction. The seat, placed where old people need one, or the street light in a dark corner where muggers had struck — small achievements like this are more *visibly* beneficial than serving on a House of Commons Committee, or taking part in a debate.

One valuable lesson I learned as a Councillor was never to trust so-called experts. They are almost always wrong. And, when you come to think about it, they permeate our lives. They tell us we must eat this, and avoid that; we should drink this and not that; we should jog for exercise; take aspirin, watch cholesterol levels and eschew spirits. But then they change their minds, and tell us exactly the opposite. Whisky makes for longevity, aspirin is bad for you, jogging can kill, cholesterol levels don't really matter much. Confusing, isn't it? Best to take no notice and do what suits you.

Northampton has a very old market square in the middle of which used to be a wonderful old Victorian wrought-iron fountain. It was the focal point of the square. We used to have meetings on the steps of it, on every eve-of-poll before a General Election. Traditionally, the sitting Member would go first, followed by the Conservative contender and then anyone else who was putting up as a candidate. Hundreds of people would flood into the market square on these occasions, and the fun was fast and furious. Insults and questions would fly; the odd skirmish might break out between rival factions, but it was all pretty good-humoured and I never saw any real trouble.

Then a panel of experts declared that the fountain was unstable and bits of it might well fall on passing members of the citizenry. It was positively dangerous! The Council might be sued, found culpable and served with a large bill. The very thought made aldermanic cheeks pale and gave Councillors the jitters.

A hotly-debated wrangle ensued. Letters flooded in to the local paper. 'Save the Fountain' committees were set up. Even John Betjeman became involved: it was, after all, just his sort of campaign. It emerged that there were only two examples of this magnificent wrought-iron work in the whole country. I was a strong and energetic supporter of the 'Save the Fountain' lobby, not only because I am a conservationist at heart but because the whole edifice seemed to me to be as solid as a rock.

Many of us argued the case passionately in the Council Chamber and outside, but the wreckers won, albeit by a narrow majority. The fountain had to go.

It took a team of 10 men and a tractor five days to budge it. It would never have fallen down in a thousand years.

Various schemes for a replacement were mooted, and there was even a competition for sculptors to design a suitable piece of statuary. One was actually selected, but there was nearly as great a row about *that* as there had been about the fountain in the first place. The empty mound left was levelled and paved. Ever since then the old market square has no focal point; and a piece of the past is gone forever.

And since then, whether the question has to do with diet, finance, weather, medicine, education, transport needs, fashion, art, religion or monuments, I have observed with sorrow that experts get it wrong nearly every time. Never trust them.

CHAPTER FOUR

Getting Nearer ...

A BOUT 18 months after I had become a Councillor, in December 1957, I was officially adopted as the first woman Prospective Parliamentary Candidate for Northampton.

The second stage on the road to my goal had been reached. True, the duties attending the first would have to be conducted in tandem with the second, but in many ways this was a 'plus'. A Councillor has many opportunities to get to know the electorate well and try to prove that he or she would make every effort to be a hardworking and caring MP. He or she also gets to know the area and its problems inside out. But there are cons as well as pros. It is distinctly awkward to have a dispute with the butcher about the price of his beef or maybe its toughness. One is liable to get button-holed with a complicated supplementary benefit problem when trying to be quick getting the shopping done. At home, one can never ever really relax in a housecoat and carpet slippers, for the doorbell can ring at any moment.

My opponent in that first Parliamentary Election had represented the town for more than 14 years. For a Labour man, Reggie Paget was rather unusual. He rode to hounds and was indeed Joint Master of the Hunt. His family were all staunch Conservatives, and wealthy. He had been to school at Eton, going on to study at Trinity College, Cambridge. As a QC, he had gained national prominence when he defended the Nazi war criminals at the Nuremberg trials in 1945.

He worked hard, was quite charming and had done so much for so many people in the Constituency that it had become unthinkable that he would ever be dislodged. Labour people voted for him because he was the Labour candidate, while a large number of Tories would vote for him as well. 'You see, Reggie's really one of us', they would say.

I fought him at two General Elections, in 1959 and 1964, but although I whittled down his majority, I failed to budge him from his perch.

On the other hand, I had learned a lot and was on target for a Parliamentary seat. Most Selection Committees looked more kindly on an aspiring candidate who had fought for the Party in difficult constituencies. It never crossed my mind to give up, although it was to take me almost 10 long years as a Parliamentary Candidate before I would finally enter Parliament.

The causes I espoused as a Parliamentary Candidate were pretty varied — abolition of Schedule A tax on houses; the establishment of a Marriage Guidance Council in the town; more help for the mentally handicapped; and an unremitting campaign against Socialist controls.

I gave strong support to Prime Minister Harold Macmillan's visit to the Soviet Union in April 1959 — a visit looked upon with less than universal favour. It was not until years later that I heard an interesting story about that visit. It seems that among the British Prime Minister's retinue was an electronics expert whose job was to check every room in which discussions were to take place among the British Delegation and ensure that no listening devices had been placed there. However, wherever they went and whatever hotel suite they occupied, the expert always found a bug. The matter was taken up with some irritation with the Russian hosts, the British pointing out that these practices were breaching not only the good rules of hospitality but of protocol as well.

As a result the Soviets promised that the dacha where the Prime Minister's party was to be housed for a relaxing weekend would definitely, but *definitely*, not have any listening devices placed in it. The weekend came. The party left for the dacha. The electronics expert did his usual check and reported that there was indeed no bug; the Russians had kept their promise. However, since the Prime Minister and the Foreign Secretary wanted to be able to discuss highly confidential matters with complete freedom, the expert was asked if he would check the dacha once more. This time he found the bug.

The Prime Minister was so angry that he announced his intention of packing and leaving at once. The Foreign Secretary and the Prime Minister's advisors begged him not to do so; it would be a diplomatic disaster, bearing in mind that important talks were still scheduled for the following week. Finally, Mr Macmillan agreed to stay. The confidential talks he wanted were conducted while walking round and round the snow-covered garden, in the freezing temperature.

It was during my time as a Prospective Parliamentary Candidate that I learned how difficult it can be to gauge the response to what one had thought, before making it, was a fairly routine speech or comment. It might never be reported and sink into obscurity for ever, or it might catch the place on fire. This can happen in Parliament, too. An MP can get up on the spur of the moment with a brief point on a Supplementary Question, and find his words making headlines in every national newspaper the next day. His only warning was that the House erupted into screams, cheers, boos or imprecations, though that certainly does not automatically lead to headlines in itself. We are a noisy bunch, and decibels are not always newsworthy.

I remember one Question Time when this happened to me, although I can't for the life of me recall the subject matter. But the astonishment on my face must have been quite comic. The next day I shared a taxi with Reggie Maudling (at that time Home Secretary) as we were both due at the same official lunch. He was a dear, comforting man, and understood my dismay at what had happened the day before and the wealth of press comment that morning, by no means all of it flattering. He said: 'We all do that sometimes, Jill. I did it once and I felt just like a fireman who aims his hose at the flames expecting water to come out, and instead out gushes petrol'.

But it had happened to me before. In one of the first speeches I made as an adopted Prospective Candidate, in January 1958 to the Young Conservatives in Kettering, I criticised the trade unions. I said they seemed to have gone sour; that their main concern was no longer the well-being of their members, but to cause industrial unrest. 'Some unions are riddled with Communists from top to bottom and they are out to make trouble', I declared roundly. In 1958 few talked like that.

The roof fell in. Correspondents with names like Realist, Proud to be a Trade Unionist and Red Makes Sense wrote to the local newspapers. They wrote to me, too, and telephoned to tell me what they thought of me. Lots of them. Yet this was at a time when public concern was awakening to the growth of strikes which were actually motivated more by politics than anything else, and Peter Sellers was about to give a brilliant exposé of the new-style trade unionism in the film 'I'm Alright, Jack'.

I was no end chuffed when a very widely-read column in a newspaper supported me. The journalist responsible, bless him, wrote: 'Mrs Jill Knight was mightily assailed when she said the trade unions had gone sour and were out to cause industrial unrest. At Birmingham, trade unionists are doing their utmost to confound Mrs Knight's detractors. In trade unionism an element of totalitarianism is apparent. The men of the giant AEU are not striking for more wages, they are striking against working with a man from another union — the National Association of Toolmakers. Some might describe the extraordinary sense of intolerance shown by this incident as industrial apartheid — but what of the national interest? Whether the vehicles not being produced will upset the trade balance matters not a whit to these strikers. Would you not say this union has "gone sour" and that its objective is to provoke industrial unrest?'

The letters and the phone calls stopped after that. But the rise in the power of the unions ground on relentlessly, and without Mrs Thatcher's single-mindedness, clarity of vision and determination two decades later, they would have brought the country down.

Addressing meetings becomes routine for Parliamentary Candidates. Sometimes the Party will provide a useful boost to status and morale by dispatching a Minister, or other worthy notable, to come and share the platform. I must say that I was fortunate in those allotted to me.

The Lord Chancellor of the day, the Right Honourable Viscount Kilmuir (who had had a distinguished career in the Commons as David Maxwell-Fyffe), was the first high ranker who came. There was a dinner in a local hotel first, then the platform party repaired to the Town Hall. Crowds still packed political meetings in the late Fifties, and we found ourselves at the back of a large number queuing to get in. We elbowed our way forward and where we were recognised, the throng parted respectfully. But it was very thick and we had quite a job to reach the doors. Once inside, we were shown to an anteroom while the audience got itself seated.

As we made our way up onto the platform, I was amazed to observe that the Lord Chancellor was shaking, as well as perspiring profusely. He was actually *nervous*! Until that moment I was perfectly happy, and looking forward to the short speech I was about to make when the great man had finished his. Golly, I thought, this man has been a Law Officer and has made the House of Commons hang on his every word; he has been a QC, and commanded immense respect for his speeches in Court. Now he sits on the Woolsack as the Lord Chancellor of England. If *he* is nervous at the thought of addressing this audience, I ought to be *paralytic*! I do not remember a single other thing about that meeting, but apparently it was quite successful.

Lord Woolton came, too. He was Chairman of the Party at that time, but he recalled his wartime job of boot controller. (That such a post even existed was news to me.) It went down very well in Northampton when he told a story which he said happened some time after the First World War, while he was in the United States. Some fairly minor accident occurred when he was travelling on a train, and he was thrown into the snow. The Americans said they must provide fresh clothing and footwear. He admitted he did need clothes, as his were soaking wet, but he said he had no need for shoes as the ones he was wearing had been made in Northampton, and his feet were perfectly dry, even after a walk of some miles to the nearest town. This created quite an impression, and the shoes were sent all round the US boot and shoe factories to illustrate the excellence of good English workmanship. His Lordship paused, walked round to the front of the platform and lifted his trousers. 'Even these were made in Northampton', he said. The applause was deafening.

Lady Isobel Barnett, who had such a big public following as a TV and radio performer, also came to speak for me. She was such a beautiful and gracious lady then, and it seemed she had only to go on being herself to bask in public affection and admiration for ever. The stress of public life, as an entertainer as well as a Councillor and Justice of the Peace in her native Leicestershire, must have affected her more than anyone realised at the time. Her life ended so sadly, dogged by mental instability and the scandal of a court case — over shoplifting, of all things. But that was later.

Iain Macleod came for me when he was Leader of the House and Party Chairman. He spoke at our Grammar School on the burning issue of the day — whether grammar schools should stay as part of our education system, or whether they should be turned into comprehensive schools. He declared: 'There is a place for great and ancient grammar schools and a place for modern efficiently run comprehensive schools, but there is no place for the insanity of killing one to provide the other'. He went on to praise what he described as an excellent comprehensive school near to his home, clearly expressing his support for it, then he continued: 'But for heaven's sake *do not* pull down what you have'. Sadly, that was precisely what they eventually did.

John Boyd Carpenter made a splendid speech on my behalf, too, when he was Minister of Pensions and National Insurance; Gerald Nabarro came — he of the handlebar moustache and gutsy, forthright attacks on the anomalies of Purchase Tax —

the things it fell on, and the identical things which it did not. He was more famous than many a Minister.

During those hectic years, I packed in an awful lot. I became Conservative Whip on the Council, responsible for ensuring that our maximum vote was achieved at every Council meeting. As numbers of Labour and Conservative were neck and neck, this was a vital task. I was involved with a large number of organisations which were outside politics, like the British Leprosy Relief Association, the Townswomen's Guild, the Royal Society for Mentally Handicapped Children and the Marriage Guidance Council. I became President of the local Old Persons' Club, the Gilbert and Sullivan Society, and the Northants Branch of the Royal College of Midwives, Chairman of the Youth Employment Committee and Chairman of two or three Boards of School Governors. A host of other appointments came my way, too. It was all extremely interesting and all the time I was learning — about people, about organisations and about politics. I toured factories, drew raffles, judged competitions, opened fêtes, art shows, offices and charitable shops. I also took part in Brains Trusts. These seem to have vanished now; they were local 'Any Questions?' sessions run by churches, Townswomen's Guilds, Round Table and other clubs — and were very popular.

But political speaking was the constant thread, and there was not a single county in England or Wales to which I did not travel for the local Conservative Association.

CHAPTER FIVE

Struggle and Success

IN the Fifties and Sixties, Northampton was still very much a boot and shoe town. This was before the era of cheap Italian shoes, and takeover bids in the industry. Enormous factories, such as Barratts, Mansfield, TrueForm and Barkers were still the lifeblood of the town. This meant that all Prospective Parliamentary Candidates, if serious about the job in hand, had to reckon to do a great deal of factory visiting. I duly went over the lot, and soon there wasn't much left for me to learn about making shoes.

The only tours I really found difficult to take were the ones over the tanneries. There, the air was inevitably loaded with the most ghastly stench imaginable. Choking, I would gasp my way along, always trying to speed up progress through the sheds, to get to the blessed fresh air in the open space between them. The amazing thing was that the manager, or whoever was showing me round, seemed never to smell a thing; he might as well have been working in a bed of roses. It turns out that people who work in any factory where there is a strong smell will not notice it at all after a day to two. I found this true in Cadbury's chocolate factory in Birmingham, which I visited some years later. The smell of chocolate, delicious for a short while, soon becomes overpowering and very sickly — yet those labouring to produce the milk and plain, the soft centres and the hard, are entirely immune to it. Whether the same miracle comes into play for those who work in an Indian take-away I have never asked — but I suppose it must.

All Councillors and Prospective Parliamentary Candidates learn a lot of lessons along the way. One phenomenon, verified many times over, is that whenever a person attains high office, some special alchemy works to bring out talents which had not been visible before. The office of Mayor is frequently (especially in the larger Councils) conferred simply on the 'Buggins' turn' rule. On occasion it has seemed that Mr So-and-So, a long-standing Councillor, will be sure to be a total disaster as a Mayor: he can't make a speech, and when he tries he is incapable of knowing when to stop. He (or she) doesn't look the part, and lacks the skill and the presence which one would suppose vital for controlling a Council successfully. Predictions of a year of disaster loom over the Mayor-making procedures. And then, lo and behold, the poor specimen will turn out to be a huge success as Mayor, confounding all critics, delighting the Press, and coping with even the worst trouble-maker with steely firmness and disarming charm.

In our Council chamber, in Northampton, Mayor-making was the pinnacle of the year. The Aldermen and Councillors were in their robes and tricorne hats. The Lord Lieutenant of the County would be there, and the MP. Two children from every school were wedged in, not always over happy at the honour, since they each had to write an essay about it all when they got back. The Public Gallery would be crammed, mostly with relatives of the incoming Mayor. This was his day. When the ceremony had been completed, and the mayoral chain was safely around his neck, the length and content of his speech of acceptance was a matter entirely for him. No-one could interrupt or silence him, nor could anybody leave until *he* did.

On one never-to-be-forgotten Mayor-making, the incoming First Citizen had decided to regale the captive audience with his life story. It began:

'I well recall the day me muther an' father came down t' Northampton. I were nobbut a young lad, an' me father came down t' look for work. There were none up North ...'.

The tale ground on, in great detail, all through school days at Campbell Square Boys' School in Northampton. We heard about when he was kept in; what his mother gave him to take for school dinner; how he had once had a catapult confiscated

by the Head. On he went: into starting work; then the actual
jobs he had to do, along with details of all the foreman's
idiosyncrasies, and even what he got up to on the works outing.
Eventually we got to the part where he met a young lady, and
starting courting. We heard where she lived. We were told the
reaction of individual members of her family to the courtship,
including an Auntie Bea and an Uncle Charlie, whose views
seemed to be most important. Uncle Charlie had a watch
chain with a gold hunter on it, and Auntie Bea's hats were a joy
to behold.

All this had taken about half an hour, and the new Mayor
was only just getting into his stride. We heard how he and
Beattie, the fiancée (she had been named after the picturesque
Auntie Bea), went for walks along the canal bank, and how he
took her to high tea at his house on Sundays. It sounded to have
been a long courtship, and it probably was, as those were still
the days of bottom drawers, and patience. At last we reached
the wedding day — which apparently dawned fine and warm.
This turned out to be an extremely good thing, because when
the bridegroom and his best man arrived at the chapel, the big
doors were locked; and despite any amount of banging and
shouting, no-one appeared to admit the advance guard. Time
wore on. Guests started to turn up. Eventually the bride made
her ceremonial appearance, 'in a lovely pink costume with a
corsidge of flowers on it'. She and her father were met by a
bemused huddle of guests, still squinting into the horizon for
signs of an approaching dog-collar.

Finally, someone went off to find the Verger, who, it
transpired, was working on his allotment. Once alerted to the
crisis, he was anxious and ready to help; he gave it as his
opinion that the Pastor would, more than likely, be at the
market, since it was a fine, bright day and he had said that he
wanted some trailing lobelia for his garden. Following up his
hunch, the Verger fetched his bike and pedalled off furiously to
the market (a journey of not much over two miles). The
enterprising fellow found the Pastor exactly where he had
predicted — happily selecting lobelia plants — and conveyed to

him the urgency of the situation. The Pastor, bundling the chosen plants into a carrier bag, rushed down the road to catch a bus. Further delay ensued, inevitably, as he had to go back to the Manse to change, but he did it at the double, and meanwhile the Verger procured a key and let the wedding party into the church. Uncle Charlie was *very* glad to sit down.

On went our new Mayor's saga, as he worked up towards his fine dramatic climax:

'Then in came t' Pastor at a trot. And finally, there on that littl' iron grille in front of the altar' [*here there was a pause for effect*] 'with all ower friends and relations looking on, an hour and an 'alf after it should've 'appened, *our marriage were consummated*'!

Those who were still awake and following this agonising story grew red from suppressed giggles, while those who had missed it woke up and asked, in a painfully audible whisper, what on earth he had said. It was a glorious moment, although I do not know what the school children made of it. However, like I said, the man turned out to be a splendid Mayor.

Since then, I have often watched ugly ducklings turn into swans, and not only on the assumption of mayoral robes. There have been jumpy Parliamentary Private Secretaries transmogrified into dignified Ministers, while dithering committee members have turned into competent chairmen. Not nearly so beneficently, I have also witnessed gentle, mild-as-milk Parliamentary colleagues galvanised into evil-tempered and terrifying bullies, after being made Pairing Whips. These unhappy men have the duty of ensuring that MPs do not leave the House when business of an important nature is coming up, or if they do, not without first obtaining a certain and sure agreement from a member of the Opposition that he or she will be away also.

But I was still a long way from learning about things of that sort in the House of Commons, and for years I seemed to get no nearer, being turned down by selection committees in a number of constituencies to which I applied.

In June 1960 I had a nice morale-boost. I was asked to move a vote of thanks to the Prime Minister — the Rt Hon Harold Macmillan — after his address to the Conservative Women's Conference at the mighty Albert Hall. He flattered me extravagantly, thus marking my card among the hundreds of constituency ladies present. This was 'getting known' in the Party, just what I needed so badly.

Then in October of that year I made a strong speech, calling for the abolition of Schedule 'A' tax on houses, at the Conservatives' Annual Conference in Scarborough. I pointed out that resolutions protesting against the tax had appeared on Conference Agendas for years, but that nothing was ever done. 'We do not put these motions down on the Conference Agenda because we are awkward, but because we believe passionately in a property owning democracy', I roared. 'This is not just a gimmick for the Conservative Party. It is a policy that is good for Britain. How can we urge people to buy their homes and then slap a tax on them for doing so?', I demanded. I took care to explain how the Chancellor could meet the £35,000,000 cost of ending the tax, too. I said that in two Budgets the tax on cosmetics had been cut from 100% to 50% and that on jewellery from 100% to 25%. 'Put some of it back — put it *all* back', I urged. 'Tax luxuries, not thrift.'

The Chancellor, however, was not to be swayed into taking my advice. 'I tell her straight', he said, 'I am not going to get involved in an argument as to whether cosmetics are a necessity or not.' However, as the *Yorkshire Evening Post* put it, 'Jill Knight roused the Conference to a high pitch of enthusiasm and left the rostrum amid a storm of applause.' There was a good deal of comment in all the national newpapers and some of them got pictures of me talking to the Chancellor on the seafront afterwards.

All this might have gone to my head, but being a mother with a family to care for, and very little money to do it on, keeps a fine old sense of proportion. Despite the generous compliments, the housework still had to be done. I still cooked, cleaned, shopped (very carefully) and washed. Oh my, *how* I washed, and by hand, at that. Our son played cricket at school and his white shirt, trousers, socks and shoes were the bane of my life. Whatever miracle powder may have been around then, the green grass stains were a devil to get out, and half my life seemed to be spent bent over the sink, rubbing like mad.

One Thursday, a small but accusing figure stumped downstairs bearing a pair of filthy cricket shoes. 'You haven't done these, Mummy, and I need them, *today*. It's games day!'

'You do them' I said. 'I have done your shirt, your trousers, your socks and your pullover.' He looked at me, with maddening male surprise at my raised tones. 'But that's what you're *for*', he said. How could I miss this simple point?

Another incident which brought me down to earth with a bump happened at the hairdressers, while I was getting spruced up for the Annual Conservative Ball. Those were the days when clients sat alone in curtained cubicles. Suddenly my attention was diverted from the pages of the magazine I was reading when I heard my name uttered, on the other side of the curtain. It was the sort of desultory conversation that goes on in hairdressing salons. Said the lady in the next cubicle:

'That Jill Knight, I don't know who she thinks she is, asking for our support. She's got no real experience at all. She may be all right as a Councillor but certainly not as an MP. I think she ought to stay home and look after her husband.'

There was a lot more in the same vein. Poor woman! When we emerged from our respective cubicles and she realised I was bound to have heard what she had said, her face was a study. She clearly longed for the floor to open and swallow her up, but I smiled sweetly at her flaming face, paid my bill and swept out. I may have been inferior, brainless, thoughtless and insignificant — but I had my dignity.

Besides, I was able to feel sorry for her because I could remember a time when *I* had wished the floor would open up for me. It was when we were first married. The winters were bitterly cold, and Monty and I both got bad chilblains on our toes. We use to sit, one on each side of a log fire, both with our feet immersed in a bowl of cold water. It was the only thing which stopped the itch, and all those who have suffered from chilblains will know exactly what we went through.

It so happened that at the peak of one of these bouts of chilblains, we were due to attend a dinner-dance. Off we went, dressed to the nines, driving through snow and ice, but much looking forward to a good meal. Throughout the initial business of checking our coats, being introduced to the rest of our party at the table, finding our places and sitting down, the itching chilblains were quiescent: my feet were too cold. But the warmth in the decorated hall, plus the first course of hot soup, started the tiresome things off with a vengeance. The itching became unbearable, and all my concentration was directed to the mental effort of stopping myself bending down for a good rub. Then — praise be — I discovered there was a table-leg only about four inches from my feet. Oh, the bliss, the joy, as I used it as a scratching-post! I concentrated on keeping my top half quite still while my legs were rubbing away under the table, and the tickle mercifully subsided. I returned to my soup, which was really awfully good, and started to take a polite interest in the other guests. It was then I noticed a lone young man seated opposite me, staring miserably down at his plate as if *his* soup, at least, wasn't up to standard. I gave him a friendly smile, to cheer him up, and asked him: 'Aren't you enjoying it?' The reaction was astounding. He turned a rich shade of beetroot, gave a strangled gulp and fled the table. I stared after him in amazement. Two minutes later I discovered to my horror that my table leg wasn't there any more!

He never came back, and so I was never able to explain. Sir, if after all these years you should just happen to read this book, I am very sorry. I am really, and it certainly wasn't what you thought.

Thank goodness such a disaster never occurred during the dinners I was beginning to attend at the House of Commons. By now — this was in the early Sixties — I was Treasurer of the Association of Adopted Conservative Candidates, having been Northampton's adopted candidate for many years. The Association held fairly frequent conferences and meetings — sometimes at a London Club, and sometimes at the Conservative College in Swinton, Yorkshire. The most regular get-togethers, however, were over dinner at the House of Commons. There we would discuss tactical problems and issues of the day, and listen to a Minister invited to speak on them.

We Prospective Parliamentary Candidates would always arrive at these dinners well ahead of time, so that we could listen to the debate in the House, from the Strangers' Gallery. This way much could be learned about the House and its rules, before we were actually elected as MPs. Although some of the friends I met there never made it to Westminister, others, like Toby Jessel, Ian Gow (brutally murdered by the IRA in 1990), Marcus Fox, Geoffrey Johnson-Smith and Elaine Kellett-Bowman, did and are friends still.

Although I had lots of political duties which took me out of the home for parts of the day, I was never away for long. Our little family was very close; success for one was success for all. The day at our local junior school when *both* the boys won a prize at the same Speech Day will remain in my memory for ever. I almost burst with pride as, in turn, they were called to the platform.

My family were as overwhelmed as I myself, when I was awarded an MBE in the New Year's Honours List of 1964. We all went to Buckingham Palace for the Investiture in March of that year. The four of us all had new suits for the occasion, though we had to explain to a dubious Andrew that brand new vests and pants were not actually essential. Her Majesty, we promised him, would never know.

Andrew always took the General Elections very seriously. He came home from school one day during a campaign and announced that he had seen 14 Mummys and only three Mr Pagets. He was talking about window bills; and he was convinced the numbers comparison meant that I was headed for victory. I had to take him to a part of town which had 10 'Mr Pagets' to one 'Mummy' so that he wouldn't be too disappointed when the inevitable happened. Roger, three years younger and rather more belligerent than Andrew, came in one day to tell me there was a 'Paget' poster in a house just round the corner. 'Do you want me to throw a stone at it, Mummy?' he inquired.

On 11 March 1965 I was adopted for the third time as Northampton's Prospective Parliamentary Candidate. However, it was with a caveat, generously offered by the Association's Officers, that if I had a chance to fight a seat where I would be more likely to win, they would release me with their good wishes. By this time I had, with the full knowledge of the Officers at Northampton, submitted myself to several Selection Committees, with no luck — up to that point.

Selection Committees are a law unto themselves. When they are in the happy position of acting for a party with a strong majority locally, their power is great indeed, and aspiring Candidates know they hold a ticket to Westminister in their gift. The actual election seems a mere formality. However, the Selection Committee itself will know that prediction is a dodgy game to play, and that they must pick someone the electorate will actually *like*. Where they fail to do this, their supposedly rock-solid seat may fall to an opposing party, causing consternation and hand-wringing — not to mention unwanted attention from the national media. This has happened enough times to make all Selection Committees nervous, and doubly so when the occasion is a By-election, and the normally dominant party is suffering a downswing in public support — as ruling parties usually do in mid-term. A seat lost like this may well remain in the opposing camp for years. It's a high price to pay for one miscalculation.

Undoubtedly, there was a general prejudice at the time against the idea of women MPs, and nervously cautious Selection Committees, aware of this, tended to reflect the anti-female bias in their selections. It was hard work for women candidates in those days, but I knew there was no way *I* would give up my goal, no matter how many committees turned me down in favour of a man.

The procedure in the Conservative Party when a sitting MP dies, or decides not to stand again, is for the local Party to set up a Selection Committee comprising all the Officers of its Association, plus representatives from all the Branches. Applications are then invited, for selection as the Prospective Parliamentary Candidate. The numbers of applicants will relate to the size of the Party's usual majority in the constituency — a safe seat makes a much better basis for a political career, and is a valuable prize. The Selection Committee meets and goes through all the applications. A 'long short list' is drawn up with perhaps 15 or 20 names chosen from the long list of hopefuls. The day is set, and the lucky 15 plus are invited to come along and make their case for being selected.

Each comes before the Committee in turn; and, I can tell you, it is a terrifying experience for the would-be Candidate. There is usually a long table, with the Selection Committee ranged down each side and the poor wretched interviewee in a chair at the end. Every eye turns critically upon him, or her, and the most daunting questions are asked, generally along the lines of: 'And *why* do you think you are the best person to represent this seat?'. If you answer one way it sounds impossibly cocky, yet if you answer the other way, it sounds as though you are far too unsure of yourself. As a result of all the interviews, the Selection Committee normally draws up a 'short short list', of about three or four people, who are invited to return at some date in the near future, to give a brief speech, on a subject of their choice. Each speech will be limited to 10 minutes or so, with a session of questions following. At the end of them all the Committee confers, and makes its decision.

The point of gladiatorial challenge by 10-minute speech had been reached in the selection process many years ago, in a constituency which shall be nameless. The four contenders for the nomination were assembled in the library of a large country house, while the Selection Committee were ready for action down at the other end of the corridor in the drawing-room.

The first man was called in. The other three, waiting in the library, could hear the muffled rise and fall of voices from the inquisition chamber. The sound continued for about 20 minutes. Contender number one returned and resumed his seat in the library. The second nervous hopeful received the call, went in, and exactly the same thing happened. Number three now made the long trek down the corridor. The hum broke out again, but this time, after some 15 minutes, a loud bellow of general laughter rang out. When number three came back he was smiling slyly and looking like the cat who had found the cream. Finally, off went number four, returning in due time without incident. Shortly afterwards the Agent came in and called number three back to the drawing-room to be told that the nomination was his.

Months later, when one of the three rejected Candidates met the victor, he could not help himself — he just *had* to ask what on earth he had said which had sparked the laugh and so clearly secured the nomination. The new MP was quite happy to explain. It seemed he had made an impassioned speech declaring his beliefs and intentions, and had expressed them in colourful detail. He gave his judgement on past policies and his hopes for future ones. Then he had paused and, looking round at his audience, said graciously: 'But of course if any of you disagree with any of this, I am quite happy to change it!'

Anyone looking for a 'safe' — or at least winnable — Parliamentary seat may well have to travel far and wide before finding one; and then the need to keep closely in touch with constituency affairs will mean either moving house, or facing long hours of regular travel. A woman with a husband and children will usually confine herself to areas which are reasonably near her home, since it is unlikely that her husband will or can uproot himself and change his job to suit hers, and she would much prefer not to disrupt the children and their schooling. Certainly, I myself felt this pull; I wanted to represent somewhere in the Midlands, and most of all I looked to Birmingham.

I had lived in Birmingham most of the time I was growing up, and so knew it well, still having school friends there who kept in touch by letters and visits. Besides, there is a uniqueness about Birmingham and its people. They are warmhearted, straight and utterly unpretentious. Birmingham is what it is and never pretends to be anything else. Why should it — it is the second most important city in the land with a long record of innovative policies in the political field; and it is an industrial centre second to none.

Early in 1965 there was to be a By-election in the Hall Green Division of Birmingham. Applications were invited for the Conservative nomination, and I eagerly put my name forward. If only I could win this one, I would become a part of Birmingham life again. But I knew the competition would be fierce, and in the event I was runner-up to Reginald Eyre. His victory was hardly surprising since he had done sterling work in Birmingham and was an Officer of the Conservative Association there. He had been active in national politics too, being Chairman of the Advisory Committee of the Conservative Political Centre in London.

In February of the following year, it looked as though there would be another By-election in Birmingham, due to the sudden death of the Member for Edgbaston, Dame Edith Pitt. She had been elected to Parliament originally in 1955 (not without a great struggle for the candidature), had served as a Minister in her time, and was respected and loved by her constituency right up to the end. Both her Doctor and a member of her family told me later that she had died quite simply from overwork, for she was unremitting in her service to Parliament, to the constituency, and to the Party. After even the most hectic of weeks involved in the business of Parliament, Dame Edith would spend entire weekends travelling the length and breadth of Britain, speaking at Conservative meetings.

For a constituency party, the sudden death of their Member is sad and a shock, but one of the least pleasant aspects is seeing the way applications to fill the vacancy pour in within hours of the announcement. It happened that Dame Edith's brother-in-law was the Chief Political Agent for Birmingham at that time, and he spoke to me later about some of those letters. Some purported to be letters of sympathy to the family, yet ended with a P.S.: 'By the way, I would be very glad to be considered as a candidate to follow Edith'!

I could not bring myself to apply until the passing of what felt to me to be a decent interval. In fact, as I was told later, my application was the last one they received. I went to see Geoffrey Johnson-Smith, who was Vice Chairman in charge of candidates at the time at Conservative Central Office. His answer, when I declared that I was most anxious for my name to be submitted to the Selection Committee, was one I shall never forget:

'No point', said he. 'They've had one woman and they won't choose another'.

Irritated by this strange one-sided logic, I pointed out with some heat that he would never say 'since this constituency has had one man, there's no point in another man applying'. I insisted that my name be added to the list; by then it had reached the staggering total of 215 applicants. From those, the Selection Committee chose the first 'long short list' of 12 names. Mine was one of the 12, and so I was through to the next ordeal — first interview.

The fateful meeting took place one Saturday in February of 1966. I drove over early for the interview, taking time to tour around the area, which had been so familiar to me. I stopped awhile outside the house where I had lived, all those years while I was growing up. It was right in the middle of the constituency. Might this be a good omen?

Struggling to conceal my nerves, I listened to questions from the Committee for an hour or more, answering as well and as honestly as I could. I left in a mood of gloomy dissatisfaction with myself: they had all been very kind, but I did not feel it had gone as well for me as the interview in Hall Green a year earlier, where I had been turned down.

Monty was waiting for me at home, mad keen to hear how I had got on. But just as I started to tell him, the phone rang. It was Keith Andrews, the Edgbaston Agent, with important instructions for me. The Committee wanted me to come over on Monday the 21st February to address 90 members of the Executive Committee. A hotel room had been reserved for me and a press conference would take place the following day. 'Is this the 'short short list', then?' I queried, suddenly rather breathless. 'No, the Committee have decided to recommend only your name to the Association', he explained. Unbelievably, far from failing at the first hurdle, I had reached the finishing line in one leap.

There was no happier woman in the whole of England that night, and Monty was so thrilled. He rushed off to retrieve a bottle of champagne which he had bought and hidden, unknown to me, just in case something like this happened. At long last I had triumphed. Or had I?

This was not to be the end of the matter. A row broke out in Birmingham, engendered particularly by the supporters of one of the disappointed candidates. There were headlines in the press: 'Stormy greeting for Jill Knight', said the *Birmingham Mail*; 'Candidate may split Tories', said the *Manchester Guardian*; 'Protests over Edgbaston candidate', said the *Birmingham Evening Mail*. The President of the Conservative Association, Alderman Harold Tyler, was very calm and dignified in the statements he gave to the press. 'The decision was practically unanimous and the meeting was a very happy one', he announced.

In the event the threatened opposition to my Candidature evaporated. To quote from a rather flowery piece written in the *Birmingham Post* on 5 March 1966:

'Mrs Jill Knight, whose selection as Prospective Conservative Candidate for Edgbaston caused a certain amount of misgiving when it was first announced, came triumphantly into her kingdom last night. A crowded Adoption Meeting, which overflowed into the adjoining hall, gave her a rapturous welcome and when the Motion was put, not a hand was raised against it.'

We had all expected a By-election but, in fact, shortly afterwards the Prime Minister, Harold Wilson, announced that a General Election would take place on the 31st March. A totally new chapter of my life was opening, as the elected Member of Parliament for Birmingham, Edgbaston.

CHAPTER SIX

Settling In

BIRMINGHAM is a remarkable city, and very much under-rated by those who have never been there. People moving to Birmingham frequently have inflicted upon them a deal of unwanted sympathy, from friends and relatives who imagine the place to be an industrial and cultural desert, where life is dull and the natives unfriendly. These friends are wrong in every particular. Some parts are drab, and pretty rough too — but show me any big city which does *not* have such blots. There are, of course, factories and chimneys; but a good deal of Birmingham is green and pleasant with spacious parks, tree-lined roads and traffic islands ablaze with flowers. There is none of the business of spending hours getting to and from work, which so many London commuters are forced to do. For most people, 20 minutes to half-an-hour will be quite enough time to get between home and their job, and indeed many people living in Edgbaston can walk to work. There are still beautiful homes, with large gardens, within a mile of the city centre.

Every sort of entertainment abounds in Birmingham, and there are top flight schools and universities, hospitals where they pioneer health techniques, shops of quality for all tastes, museums, art galleries, one of the finest concert halls in the world, libraries and even an ancient stately home (Aston Hall) — and all within easy reach of the most delightful countryside. The Royal Ballet and the D'Oyly Carte Opera are now based in Birmingham; and the City of Birmingham Symphony Orchestra, under the baton of the brilliant and highly-regarded Sir Simon Rattle, is known and admired all over the world. A move to Birmingham calls for congratulation, not commiseration.

This is the place I have had the great good fortune to
represent in Parliament, for nearly 30 years now; and when I
began there was the added bonus of going back to the place I
knew so well, and renewing old friendships. It was like going
home.

The Houses of Parliament took rather more exploration before I
could feel at home there. The Palace is so *huge*. There are miles
of corridors, the main ones book-lined with chandeliers
hanging from 30-foot ceilings. Walk the length of one, turn the
corner, and there facing you is an identical long corridor, its
walls similarly book-lined, its chandeliers an exact copy of the
ones you have just left behind. The first time I ventured down
them I felt just like Alice in Wonderland, and such was the
sense of unreality that I half-expected to see the White Rabbit
pop out from one of the doors set among the bookshelves and
give me some agitated instructions.

Like Alice, I felt I must examine the doors, too. One
was labelled in gold Gothic characters, 'Members only'. I
thought, 'Well, I'm a Member' and opened it. Embarrassingly, I
found that it should have been labelled 'Gentlemen Members
only'!

Facilities for Lady Members were more rare; there were not
very many of us, anyway, but I did think, since some 40 years
had elapsed since Lady Astor entered the place as the first
woman Member to do so, that the men's lavatories might have
been properly marked. Twenty-four years on, the notices still
hadn't been changed, though they have now. But they don't
rush things in the Palace of Westminster.

In 1966 there were very few desks available for Members,
and certainly no offices; it was a matter of just working where
there was space. I recall taking a party of schoolchildren round
one morning and coming across Enoch Powell replying to his
letters at a desk in the 'No' lobby, as we all passed by. But
women did have some advantage over men in this regard: I

was told I could find a spare desk in the Lady Members' Room on the Terrace.

At that time the Lady Members' Room was ruled with a rod of iron by no less a personage than Mrs Bessie Braddock, the bulky and fiery Member for Liverpool Exchange. She had once been a member of the Communist Party, a fact she never took the trouble to disguise; and indeed, one of her claims to fame was that she had actually danced on the floor of the House while it was in session — this presumably being the only way she could sufficiently express her joy at the landslide Labour victory of 1945. But it was now 21 years later, and she had altered so much that she was practically a Conservative. Certainly she would have found no compatibility whatever with the Labour Party of the 1990s. In any event, she was always immensely kind to me, in her bluff Liverpudlian way, very much the Grande Dame. I admired and liked her.

When I entered the Lady Members' Room on that first April morning, she returned my greeting with: 'Hello, luv. Your desk will be that one over there.' I went to the desk she indicated, but it seemed to be already booked. 'Mrs Braddock' I said diffidently, 'there's a card on it and it says Miss Joan Lestor.' Bessie threw out her not inconsiderable chest and snorted angrily, 'It says *what*?' Snatching the card from me, she tore it across first once, then twice — and hurled it into the waste-paper basket. 'She can go upstairs wi' the left-wingers if she likes', she said. 'She's not coming in here!'

I should have loved to have been at my desk when Miss Lestor entered to claim it. Alas I was not, and so cannot report what Bessie said to her, but in all the years that Miss Lestor sat in the House (and she later returned after some years away) I never saw her in that room, even long after Bessie was dead and gone.

It was at that desk I struggled to answer by hand all the letters from kind people who wrote to congratulate me. One was from Bedford Gaol. It read thus:

'Dear Mrs Knight,

'I am ever so pleased you got into Parliament at last. I live in

Northampton when I am not in here and I've always voted for
you. I had to write and congratulate you.

'Yours sincerely,

....

'P.S. We're all Conservatives in here.'

I hoped this was more an indication of the entrepreneurial bent
of the inmates than evidence of general villainy among
Conservative voters. Still the letter amused me greatly.

A major problem for those newly-elected to Westminster is
finding accommodation in London. I promptly became a
member of a Ladies Club. The establishment I chose, which
was in Grosvenor Street, had a solemn and dignified character
all its own. It was mainly inhabited by elderly ladies from the
country who wore their hair up (in rather wispy buns) and
their skirts down, flapping unfashionably around their lace-up
shoes. I recall particularly the cavernous dining room, and the
breakfasts served there, which comprised thin burnt toast and
an unpleasant dark brown liquid which had not the slightest
resemblance to any coffee I had ever encountered. If piped
Musak had been around then, the place would have been filled
with the strains of mournful dirges from the gloomier composers.
As it was, we nibbled our toast audibly amidst the pillars and the
portraits. Still, that Club provided me with a London home for a
whole year at a reasonable cost, for which I was grateful.

In those days it was possible for me to park my car outside,
and give the Night Porter a sixpence to put in the parking meter
at half past eight in the morning. By this means I was assured of
legitimate parking up to 8:45 a.m., by which time I needed to be
off anyway. It may, I suppose, have constituted illegal meter-
feeding, but it was a handy solution to a tricky problem. My
helper, the Night Porter, was exactly like a retired Bishop,
portly and silver-haired, with a stately demeanour which
inspired confidence.

At first all went well. I would turn up for the night at the decent hour of 10:00 or 10:30 p.m. The Bishop would smile benignly at me as he received my sixpence. Then we got into a series of very late sittings on Budget debates, and I began coming in later and later. Midnight, 1:00 a.m., and (shock horror!) *past 2:30*. The later I became, the higher the ecclesiastical eyebrows ascended the domed forehead. What *was* this young women, apparently quite alone, up to until this hour?

I have never been one to explain my calling at the drop of a hat, but it was clear that some very nasty suspicions on that score were troubling the pastoral mind. I tried bringing in copies of *Hansard* and other Parliamentary papers and placing them carefully on the desk right under his nose, while I fumbled for my sixpence. That didn't work and the next night I came in at 4:30 a.m. He gave me a look which was part accusation and part leer. The time had come for plain words. 'Look', I said, 'I expect you think it very odd that I should come in so late, but I am a Member of Parliament and we are going through some very late sittings indeed.'

He grappled with this unlikely explanation, and I saw it sink in. Then another expression, this time one of extreme caution, crossed his priestly features. 'Er ... which Party, Madam?', he inquired. Luckily for me he must have been a Conservative supporter, for once I gave him his answer his manner changed completely. He beamed, he relaxed, and thereafter whenever I was late home and the night was cold, I found a hot water bottle in my bed.

One night, however, I returned to the Club just as the morning light was breaking, to find the doors locked; and though I rang and knocked for a long time, no-one came. There was nothing for it but to go over the railings into the basement area and clamber on the dustbins, from which I could just reach the edge of a window which I had noticed was fractionally open. As I wriggled in over a sink and some saucepans (this was the kitchen I was entering) I thanked my lucky stars that there were no Press cameramen about. I tiptoed in the half-light past piles of plates, enormous enamel food containers and some strange looking steel machines, through a baize door, up the stairs and past the Bishop — fast asleep in his chair. I unhooked my key silently from the board and crept up to bed.

Soon after that I found a tiny house in Lambeth which I rented from the Prince of Wales, for this was Duchy of Cornwall property. I was a little sorry to say goodbye to the Bishop, but it was good to put some roots down: not to have to pack everything up at the end of each week and take it home, only to lug it back again the following Monday. Besides, it meant Monty and the boys could come and stay over when anything special was happening.

My little house was in a friendly Cockney street. One day I returned there, clutching my newly-repaired vacuum cleaner, which I put down on my doorstep while I fumbled with my key. I found it, put it in the door, and turned it. Obligingly making the half turn, it became obstinate at the final segment, and stuck fast.

Patiently I tried again . . . repeatedly . . . for about 20 minutes. By this time quite a little crowd of helpful passers-by had gathered to offer advice and try the key. They were as unsuccessful as I had been.

A passing plumber gave his verdict: 'What you've done', he said accusingly, 'is to put the little lever down at the top of the lock. She won't budge while that's on.' I explained that I hadn't got that sort of lock, and nothing like that could possibly have happened. The lookers-on were openly sceptical. 'Tell you what', said a man in a bowler hat, 'let's push the cleaner plug through the letterbox and swing it round. It might just knock the lever off.' This would have been the lever I don't have — I am sure you follow perfectly.

The scientific imagination of the crowd was gripped. I could see there was no point in trying to stop them, so I hovered at the back while this scheme was put into operation. It didn't work. I knew it wouldn't.

An adventurous section of the crowd suggested going on the roof. I said there weren't any skylights. They said I might have left a window open upstairs at the back. I said I hadn't. But a ladder appeared and one pioneering spirit clambered aloft. He called down that there weren't any windows open at the back.

A fierce argument then developed as to which window had better be broken. One faction favoured the front window because the panes were smaller, but others thought it better to break a back window — 'where it wouldn't show'. The roof roamer declared that the bathroom window would be best, and volunteered to go up and do it. A hammer was produced and he swarmed up the ladder with it like an experienced cat-burglar.

At that moment, a man, who had just joined the crowd, asked if he could have a shot at turning the key. Ribald laughter greeted him from all sides. A dozen voices assured him the feat was quite impossible. Undaunted, he came up and tried the lock. And beneath our stunned gaze, he turned the key, the full distance. Just as the door swung open, the sound of breaking glass greeted us from upstairs. The crowd melted away. I tried to give the climber something for his pains, but he would not take it.

CHAPTER SEVEN
Next Please!

A TRULY extraordinary fact about an MP's job is the endless variety of the problems one is expected to solve.

When we do our constituency Surgeries, there is no knowing what we will be faced with, as the constituent is ushered in. The problem could be housing, taxation, social security, council tax, the neighbours' dog, lack of a regular bus service or not being able to get a hip operation until next year.

A constituent once came to see me because he wasn't allowed to keep an ancient car number on his ancient car; another wanted sponsorship for the London Marathon; a third asked for better street lighting, while a fourth's son was held in Marrakesh on a drug-running charge.

The problems of human beings are as diverse as their characters. There are funny ones, sad ones, tragic ones and complicated ones. There is the pathetic soul who has got himself hopelessly into debt, the intellectual who has a technical point he claims has been missed in a Select Committee study, and the steady citizen who has been hog-tied by bureaucracy. And there is absolutely no telling which will come up next.

It is not uncommon to have a grandmother whose only daughter has died and who longs to see her grandchildren regularly, but barriers are constantly put in her way by the children's father, her ex son-in-law, and his new wife.

There is the family of a gentlemen currently detained at Her Majesty's expense, who want him in Winson Green prison instead of Parkhurst because visiting is so expensive. It is a long journey from Birmingham to the Isle of Wight.

There are the parents of a child who has been allocated a

place at School B instead of A, which was the one they asked
for. And awareness of 'rights' of one kind or another can throw
up some very unusual demands indeed.

One day a young lady of about 17, with extremely blonde
curls and large, innocent blue eyes, entered my office. Across
her bosom, a tee shirt at least three sizes too small announced,
in undulating letters: 'I'M ONLY HERE FOR THE BEER.' She
sat down and crossed her legs, her mini-skirt surging well up
towards her thighs in the process. I asked what I could do to
help her.

'It's me shoes', she said. I was puzzled.

'Shoes?' I asked. 'What seems to be the matter with your
shoes?'

'They let water, don't they? I only wore 'em twice, and the
second time they let water. It's not right', she said.

She dived into a carrier bag, produced the offending shoes
and placed them squarely on the desk in front of me. I
examined them carefully. Not for nothing had I spent 10 years
as a Conservative Candidate in a town whose principal
industry was shoe-making.

'Do you mind telling me how much you paid for these
shoes?' I asked.

'£1.50', she declared.

Since this was at a time when a pair of shoes cost at least
£15.00 (Oh happy day!), I then had to spend 10 minutes
of my time explaining to her that since she only paid £1.50 it
was a miracle the shoes did not leak the *first* time she put
them on.

But I conceived a growing resentment, fuelled by incidents
of this kind, against what became known as the consumer
lobby. My idea of consumer protection is that it should be
illegal to manufacture flammable nightdresses for children, or
that toymakers should not be allowed to make soft cuddly
animals with glass eyes on sharp steel pins, or put lead-
poisonous paint on bricks that a child could bite. I do not think
that Members of Parliament should have to tell people that
very cheap items may not be the best things to spend

one's money on. The principle of *caveat emptor* is a sound one.

The girl with the shoes was much easier to deal with, though, than a man who had served in the 1939-1945 war. He told me he could not stand up properly because of what the doctors had done to him while he was a soldier.

'Look at this!', he cried, and with rapid dexterity he yanked off his socks and placed both feet on my blotter. The second toe had been amputated on each foot. Apparently both toes had bent permanently over the big toe, and some idiot of a doctor had decided to solve the problem by chopping the two bent ones off. It so badly affected his ability to balance that he had to have a medical discharge. Dear God! Is that what MOs did in the Army? He had never walked normally since, and he had come to me to investigate the possibility of a pension which, to my mind, he richly deserved.

Alas, the Army pension scheme does not work like that. Had he complained 20 years ago, he could have had one. As it was, too much time had passed.

Another case which I shall never forget began when a motherly middle-aged lady entered my office, weighed down by two carrier bags from the local supermarket.

'Please sit down, Mrs Blank. How can I help you?'.

She sat down heavily with one bag on each side and gazed at me, a rather bewildered frown on her brow. 'I don't know quite where to begin', she said.

I suggested encouragingly that the beginning might be a good place, and with pen poised to take down the details, I waited.

'Well, all right', hesitantly. 'You see, it's like this. Me and Sid (that's my husband) had two little girls. My Sylvia was first, and then Gloria. They were as different as chalk and cheese.' (She was getting into her stride.)

'My Sylv was never a bit of trouble and such a pretty child. I remember I used to put her in lovely little white socks and when she came home from school, Mrs Knight, them socks were as neat and white as when she left in the morning. My Glor has always been quite different. When she had white socks on, they was filthy within 'arf an hour. Happened every time.'

At this point, I was on the verge of pointing out that MPs have really very little power to influence the dirtiness of socks. But I decided that now the flow was under way, I'd be better not to interrupt it. It continued ...

'It was like that all the time they was growing up. Never a scrap of bother with my Sylv. She did what she was told. She done well at school, too — but Glor was trouble from the word 'go'. She didn't work at school, she had the most awful friends, and my husband Sid and me used to have loads of arguments wiv 'er, about everything, like.' She went on to give me details of the subject-matter of some of the arguments. My note-taking hand was getting cramped by now, and I couldn't see where the story was leading at all. I tried gently to suggest that she move on to the purpose of her interview with me. 'Well, you said to start at the beginning', she said accusingly. 'I'm only trying to put you in the picture, like.'

She journeyed on through the girls' teenage years, and reached the point where both were to be married. Sylv's husband was a paragon of virtue. Steady, reliable and such a *nice* boy. He worked at the Post Office. Running true to form, Glor's intended was awful. 'One of them punk sorts, y'know — and violent with it. I won't say 'e isn't good-lookin', but Gawd, what an awful temper!'

The weddings both took place as planned, and, with a bit of encouragement from me, we passed quite quickly through the acquisition of families — Sylvia's two little girls and Gloria's girl and boy. They all lived quite near to each other, and the children were by now all at school, except for Sylv's youngest, who was only three.

'But what is the *problem*?', I wailed, patience wearing thin as I contemplated the numbers undoubtedly gathering in the waiting room outside. 'I'm telling, I'm *telling* you', she said, in an injured tone. 'Last night my Gloria's husband murdered my Sylvia's husband.'

Whatever I expected, that wasn't it. I was speechless.

'Sid said best go and see Mrs Knight about it. She'll know what to do.'

I inquired shakily whether they had called the police. 'Course we done *that*', she said scornfully. (Had Sid's trust been misplaced?)

'But what will 'appen to the children? There's Glor's 'usband in prison and Sylv's 'usband dead. My girls can't be expected to cope in a situation like that! What can you do about the children? The money and that, with no wages coming in?'

Ashamed of my unsympathetic abruptness earlier, I gave her all the information I could about what benefits would be available to her daughters, and offered to do whatever might be possible with the DHSS on their behalf.

This constituent was tall, broad, brown and dignified. He wore flowing robes and entered the room slowly, palms pressed together. He hoped blessings would fall on me, my house and my family. I invited him to sit down but he preferred to stand. I had some difficulty in getting him off the blessing and on to the subject of his problem. Finally he reached it. His problem was his beautiful daughter. I remarked that I understood that it was not unusual that beautiful daughters meant problems, but what were his? And why was I anything to do with them?

The girl was now 27 years of age. It was time she married. There was disgrace in reaching such an age still living, unwed, in the home of her father. I was puzzled. If the girl was so beautiful, surely suitors should be queueing at her door. Was she spectacularly choosy? Did she have bad breath? Did she keep dangerous pets? I mused while her father talked on.

It seemed that, for religious reasons, she must marry with a boy of their own sect. I remarked encouragingly that there were plenty of such boys in Birmingham. Well, yes, that was true.

Unfortunately, on two occasions now a marriage had been arranged with a suitable local boy, but when the couple were introduced, the young man decided he did not wish to marry her. I failed to see how I was supposed to be able to help. Did he expect me to mix him a potion?

No, no; it was simpler than that. All he asked was that I would make it possible for a young man of the right religion to come into the UK, from their country of origin, so as to marry her. This would solve the problem. They would select the candidate, and my part in it would be to intercede with the Home Office, who were known to be difficult in such matters, but would doubtless listen to me. The wedding could take place the moment the plane landed, and the couple could settle down to a happy life in Birmingham, filled with blessings and bathed in goodwill.

That was his scenario. I didn't buy it. If the girl was as lovely as the father claimed, I was sure a suitable bridegroom must be available nearer to hand. I said as much. He stared at me regretfully. Then, like a conjuror producing a rabbit from a hat, he waved his arm, and his daughter — who had been standing hidden behind him all this time — was suddenly on view.

I gazed at her, astounded. She was certainly beautiful. Her face was a perfect oval and her long, black hair, shining and smooth as silk, fell to her waist.

There was just one thing wrong. One only had to look at her for a moment to see that she was hopelessly mentally handicapped. Her gorgeous eyes were quite, quite empty.

I became very angry. This man expected me to connive at saddling some poor wretched young man with a mentally incapable wife. Get him over to Britain with the lure of a dowry and a new home, and have him marry the girl, probably veiled (shades of Henry VIII and Anne of Cleves), before he realised what he was doing.

I told him roundly I would not have any part in his scheme. His reaction made me angrier still. He clapped his hand to his head. 'Oh, I am so stupid!', he said, 'I have forgotten to give you the present!' With that he grabbed a parcel which the girl had been holding and started to unwrap it.

'Please stop doing that' said I. 'I never accept presents of any kind from constituents.' Still pulling off pieces of paper and scattering them liberally round my office, he assured me I would like the present very much. It was known that I had visited the Khyber Pass on more than one occasion. This came from the Khyber Pass. 'I don't care where it comes from,' I bellowed, 'I don't want it!' 'But it cost much money', he said, still tearing the paper off. 'I don't care what it cost, *I shall not accept it*.' My bellow had turned to a roar. But at that moment, the last scrap of paper was removed, and he placed the present proudly on the desk in front of me.

Horror of horrors! It was a *stuffed snake*!

I hate snakes of any kind. This one was a cobra, and it was wound, in its frozen pose, round the body of a wretched little mongoose, which stared at its attacker with baleful eyes — surrealistic glass eyes. The thing was, to put it kindly, quite horrid, and my voice rose a good octave in one leap as I shrieked at him: 'Get that thing out of my room, NOW!!'

I don't know which infuriated me more, the belief that I would be prepared to ruin the life of a young man on request, or the assumption that I had to be given a present to do my job of helping constituents.

But he got the message, and the last I saw of him was his retreating form, daughter under one arm and snake under the other, vanishing through my Surgery door.

A colleague tells of a tall, angular woman with large hands, red hair and feather earrings who flounced into his office, but seemed attacked by doubt once seated in the Surgery chair.

He asked, encouragingly, how he could be of assistance.

'Well', said she, 'I've had a sex-change.' He told her hastily that he had no medical knowledge whatever and that if she was having trouble with her sex-change, she must go and see a doctor. It was a different sort of Surgery she needed.

'No, no, you don't understand', she said. 'My sex-change has been a *complete* success. I have no problems at all over my *operation.*'

'Oh good. Great. I'm very pleased to hear it', said the MP. There was a pause. 'Er, if there is no problem with the operation, what is the difficulty and how can I help?'

'Well', she said, 'I used to be a man, right?.' 'Er, if you say so', said my poor colleague, wondering what on earth was coming next.

'And now I'm a woman, right?' she declared. He gazed thoughtfully at the feather earrings and agreed.

'Well, am I going to get my pension when I'm 60 or 65?', she asked.

He took refuge in the stock reply given by every politician who doesn't know the answer. 'What a very good question!', he said. He told her frankly that he had never encountered the query before, that he did not know the official position on the matter, but promised to find out and let her know.

He wrote to the Secretary of State for Social Security. He explained the situation to which Miss Thingamy had been transported, and he asked about her pension entitlement. His letter threw the whole Department into a state of frenzy. Here was a serious problem indeed. The whole economy of the country could be torpedoed if a significant proportion of the male population were enabled to claim full pension five years before they were actuarially entitled to do so. Besides, think of the drain on NHS resources if a flood of 59-year-old men demanded sex changes!

Weeks went by. Civil Servants at the Elephant and Castle feverishly sought a feasible answer, no doubt with wet towels wrapped around their heads. Finally, Miss Thingamy took to going into the MP's constituency office to complain that she had asked him for help and information and he had totally failed to produce either.

He wrote a stiff note to the Secretary of State pointing out that it was now two-and-a-half months since he had written about a constituent's problem, and, apart from an acknowledgement postcard, he had heard nothing.

An official telephoned with apologies. The issue raised far-reaching implications. It was complicated to resolve but they were getting to a conclusion. He would have an answer within the next 10 days.

The answer, when it came, was straight out of the script of a 'Yes, Minister!' television episode.

'We have considered most carefully the inquiry of your constituent Miss Thingamy (formerly Mr Thingamy), who wishes to know at what age she will be able to draw her pension. Since we note she is only 43, we do not think there is any urgency in furnishing her with a reply.'

There was, however, a far more definitive answer which later emerged. Whatever the sex on your birth certificate, that is the sex you remain for the purpose of such things as pension entitlement. Whatever happens, nothing can change your birth certificate. The point will in time become irrelevant anyway, if the Equal Opportunities Commission and the European Community succeed in equalising the age where men and women start to draw their pension.

Elderly people form a high, and increasing, percentage of the visitors to our Surgeries — not surprisingly, as the population itself ages. Many times pension problems will be the reason for their visit, though by no means always. Pensioners tend to suffer from all kinds of awkward problems and difficulties, which they hope we can sort out. A change in their accommodation needs often brings them in; the proposed closure of a nearby chemist may cause severe problems, since many need regular medication, and have no-one to bring it to them. Rude and/or noisy neighbours are a pest to anyone, but the old are often stuck with no means of escape, no way to retaliate, and perhaps no friend to turn to. The closure or deviation of a bus route can be a disaster for them, too, leaving them more than ever stranded in their homes.

On one occasion, my reception staff saw an elderly couple

coming slowly towards the office, to keep a Surgery appointment. The girls hurried out to help the couple up the steps to the door and into my office. The old lady had a Zimmer frame, and the old man shuffled along with the aid of two sticks. When they were ushered in, it was the husband who did the talking — all of it. Nellie never uttered: she fixed an unwavering, basilisk-like stare at the wall, and that was that. I asked what was their problem, and the old boy announced huskily, in quavering tones, that Nellie couldn't manage the shopping or the cooking any more, poor dear, and could they please be put in sheltered accommodation? He and his wife had struggled along as best they could, but now they simply couldn't cope any more.

I said, as gently as I could, that, if the problem was Nellie's inability to get out to the shops and do the cooking, it wasn't sheltered accommodation they wanted, because in such places pensioners still did their own shopping and cooking — it was just that they lived in a bungalow or flat which was linked by a special intercom to a Warden so that they could get immediate help if their medical condition worsened, or some accident happened. I said that I felt he and Nellie really needed to go into an old person's home, where they could be looked after, with regular meals provided, and shopping and cleaning done for them.

The old man appeared rather dubious, but said he supposed that would do. He was obviously still worried so I inquired whether he felt that perhaps they would not be able to be together in such a place. I said there were some which did take married couples, and I was sure that, if that was the difficulty, it could be overcome — though I did add that it might take some time to find a suitable home.

Concluding, from the husband's hoarse though tepid sounds of vague agreement, that we were reaching a satisfactory conclusion, and failing to get any negative response (or any response of any kind, for that matter) from Nellie, I started to take down the particulars, and asked for their ages. 'Well,' wheezed the marital spokesman, 'I am 56 and Nellie is 53.'

Wow! The poor biddies were both younger than I was! How I failed to laugh outright I'll never know, but I somehow smothered my amusement and explained that, if that was all they were, it would be some time before they would be eligible for places in an old people's home.

After they left, I asked my reception staff how old they thought the couple would be. Unhesitatingly the verdict was: 'Oh, somewhere in their eighties.' It just went to confirm another suspicion I have had for many years — figures on a birth certificate are a most unreliable guide. I have known elderly people of 27 and young ones of 80. Having no disablement problem, I'm afraid that Nellie and her husband are still awaiting their place in an old people's home.

Another memorable surgery case was the man who had been on holiday with his wife, to the Isle of Man. At some stage during the stay, the wife had a heart attack and died. For a fleeting moment I thought he was going to make an official complaint about her hospital treatment, a late ambulance or his inability to find a doctor quickly enough.

Nothing of the kind! What he wanted was a refund of the return half of her ticket, from British Rail. He saw the expression on my face and said, defensively, 'Well, it cost a lot to get her back to Birmingham.' I had an almost uncontrollable urge to remark that I didn't know why he hadn't propped her up in the corner of the carriage and proffered her ticket when the collector came round, explaining that she felt a little unwell. With an effort, I kept my mouth shut, and dutifully wrote to British Rail's Customer Service Department.

It turned out that the ticket had been a cut-price concessionary fare, and wasn't refundable. But I did get him a refund on the special annual pensioner's ticket, so all was not lost.

The most moving surgery encounter I ever had was following the unhappy experience of being burgled at my small house in Lambeth. An elderly neighbour who held my key was duped into giving it to two strangers who had knocked on her door to ask for a drink of water. (The police warn about such people all the time, but Mrs Gent 'never thought they were crooks — they spoke so nice.') All my jewellery was stolen.

This was reported at some length in the press, and the following Friday an Asian constituent whom I had been able to help earlier made an appointment to see me.

He waited patiently with all the others, clutching a plastic bag from a local supermarket. When his turn came he entered my office and put the bag on the table in front of me.

I greeted him and asked how I could help him.

'My wife and I', he said, 'read in the paper that wicked people had taken all your beautiful things. We were so sad. We talked about it and we agreed that I should bring you my wife's jewellery. She wants you to have it.'

With a lump in my throat, I explained, as gently as I could, that *of course* I could not take the lovely gold bangles, necklaces and earrings he had emptied out of the bag onto my desk. I had to be extremely firm before he would take them back, but, as I told him, he had certainly made me feel a great deal better.

There are many times when one draws strength and comfort from the human goodness and caring love of the ordinary people who flock into Surgery, or write or phone in. At a time when moral standards seem, on the face of it, so low, when wives and husbands are betrayed and children abandoned, when clergymen, civil servants, politicians and footballers are accused of taking bribes or behaving in a thoroughly dis-honourable way, I think of the many, many good, kind and honourable people I meet in the course of my work. While there *are* bad and ill-principled people who steal, cheat and lie, and act with viciousness and venom, the overwhelming majority of our citizens are honest, responsible and law-abiding people.

CHAPTER EIGHT

Bullies and Bureaucrats

ANYONE with a basic training in Local Government soon becomes conscious of the need to examine both sides of even the simplest case, before making a judgement on a complaint against an Official or a Department. The majority of Local Government staff carry out their jobs courteously, conscientiously and even-handedly. But there are bad exceptions, and these can be very serious — particularly when, as they so often do, they affect the whole quality of people's lives. The worst case of official carelessness and indifference I ever knew led to almost two years of sheer misery for a number of innocent elderly people.

It all began, so far as I was concerned, on a foggy winter's night when a group of these people came to my Friday Surgery. They were both worried and upset. They complained that a 17-year-old problem boy with a record of theft and violence had been allocated a two-bedroomed flat in the quiet Council tower block in which they lived. Although he had not yet moved in, they knew a good deal about him because one of their number had a son who worked at a local Community Home, and had learned all about this particular lad and his history.

The group explained to me that their block was a very quiet one, with everyone living peaceably together. They felt that such a place would be quite wrong for a lad of the reported type, and they feared their future calm would be shattered if he came to live among them. Could I please prevail upon the Council to put him somewhere more suitable?

The boy (we will call him John, though that is not his name) had been a resident of an Approved School, before the name of such places was changed to the more ambiguous 'Community Home'. Within a short time of the change in nomenclature,

71

these places were finally abolished altogether. The closure of John's establishment rendered him homeless, and the Housing Department in Birmingham received, from the Social Services Department, an application for housing for John, with an undertaking that the Department would guarantee his rent. They also stated that they would be keeping an eye on him as he had never lived alone before, and there were obviously a number of things he would need to learn, such as shopping and cooking for himself and keeping his flat clean.

But the fact remained that John's previous history was not good, and he had come from an Approved School. One might have thought in these circumstances that John, since he had to be allocated *somewhere*, would perhaps be offered a small bed-sitting room or a one-bedroomed flat in some convenient area of the City where Social Services could keep an eye on him.

Not a bit of it! The boy was invited to choose which area of the City he wanted to live in, and indeed one flat which became vacant was not offered to him because it was not in an area he favoured.

The second flat John turned down himself, because he did not like the look of it, but he was finally allocated a two-bedroomed flat on the first floor of the block in Quinton from which my elderly constituents came. Their fears had become fact.

Apart from their objection to the type of boy he was reported to be, the residents had a reasonable complaint in that many of them had repeatedly asked to be allowed to have two-bedroomed flats. Such flats were rather rare and extremely desirable for people who had relatives whom they would wish to invite to stay. My tenant constituents had always paid their rent, and never caused a scrap of trouble to anyone, and they found it most unjust that their request for a two-bedroomed apartment should have been turned down time and again by the Housing Department, whereas this boy with all his background, and with his total lack of experience in managing a one-bedroomed flat (let alone a two-bedroomed one) should instantly have been offered what *they* had been requesting for many years, to no avail.

The Housing Department were perfectly well aware of the character of the block, and the kind of tenants that lived in it. Oddly enough, the Housing Committee was at that very moment considering converting the whole block to Warden-assisted accommodation, catering particularly for the problems of the elderly people housed there.

To place a 17-year-old boy from an Approved School in such a block was about as appropriate as putting the proverbial bull in the well-known china shop.

After a long talk with the residents' deputation, I wrote a detailed letter to the Council conveying the tenants' concerns and enclosing a petition signed by every single person in the block.

This letter was completely ignored. In fact, as they later admitted, the Council promptly lost my letter *and* the petition, and did nothing whatever about either.

The worst fears of the residents were realised with astonishing speed and accuracy. Noisy parties began on the very night that John moved in, and after that there were two or three every week. Reggae and pop music blared out mercilessly, starting at around 10:30 or 11:00 in the evening and continuing until four or five in the morning. There was a great deal of thumping as the youngsters present danced, and a great deal of shouting and screaming, too. Scores of young people congregated in the hall and on the stairways, frightening and upsetting the elderly residents. Whether John deliberately tried to upset his neighbours, or merely acted according to his normal habits, is difficult to say. But urinating on the stairs was another of his less lovable traits.

He had a motorbike, although nobody quite knew how this had been acquired or paid for, since John was unemployed and living on Social Security benefits. He took this motorbike up to his first-floor flat, where he garaged it, and occasionally started it up. The bike was the subject of another spate of complaints.

John had painted the whole of the interior of this flat jet black, and it became a centre for a large number of youngsters in the area. Most were younger than John — some only 11 or 12 years old. They knew there was absolutely no discipline of any kind there, and they could do exactly as they wished while in John's flat; so its attractions were enormous.

All sorts of 'games' and dares took place. Some of the teenage visitors would jump from John's first-floor balcony on to the ground beneath, risking life and limb, and greatly alarming the tenants in the ground-floor flats. John lost his keys, so he forced the entrance door to the flats, effectively ending all the security on which the elderly tenants relied.

When the Caretaker reported these problems to the Housing Department and the Social Services office, he was told to 'mind his own business'.

The tenants became regulars at my Surgery and their letters were numerous in my postbag. Quite apart from the constant stream of complaints from the tenants and the Member of Parliament (for I always wrote to the Housing Department officials to convey complaints as they came in), Local Government officials had their own indication that all was not well. One such Officer was to explain later that during this period he called on John on numerous occasions, leaving a card behind him on each visit, which asked John to contact him. John ignored every card, and no contact was ever made. The Housing Department remained deaf to all complaints and took no action whatsoever.

The police were called frequently; there were constant disturbances at all hours of the day and night and several of the older tenants were literally ill with the worry and the noise. One had a heart attack, and two had strokes. In a situation like this, there is only one shot left in the locker, and I had to use it. I contacted the local press. The story became headline news, and at last local Officials sat up and took notice.

But by now John was over 18, and evicting him was no easy matter. The law was on his side in spite of everything. A Notice was served seeking possession of the flat, but John avoided bringing the case to a conclusion by the simple expedient of ignoring all Summonses to Court.

By this time, the tenants themselves had formed an

Association, and employed a solicitor. He wrote to the City Housing Officer and, making no bones about it, warned that 'unless the Council take steps to remove John from occupation, an action is to be begun on behalf of John's neighbours to compel the Council to remove him on the basis that the Council is in breach of its covenant to permit neighbouring tenants to live "in quiet enjoyment of the dwelling"'. The Council's reply was that they were doing what they could, but were 'constrained in providing the early solution preferred by your clients by the due process of law'. The tenants referred the case to the Local Government Ombudsman and he agreed to undertake an investigation.

Meanwhile John was in trouble for another reason, having been charged with a number of burglaries; and house-breaking tools had been found by the Police in his flat. Faced with this evidence the Court calmly released him on bail, *on condition that he continue to live at the flat.* (My italics.)

Bearing in mind all the sorry history of this case, and the efforts that were being made at the same time to get John out of the flat, I found that Court ruling as incredible as anything in the list of incredible happenings in this case. The Council's Legal Officers thought it unlikely that they would be granted possession of the flat while the bail conditions applied, so there was further delay while they waited until the criminal charges had been dealt with.

By the time John had been forced to vacate the flat, and peace descended on the block once more, 19 months of fear, harassment and noise had been inflicted on a number of people who deserved better from their Council landlord.

It was the Local Government Ombudsman who revealed in his findings that my initial letter and petition from the residents had been lost and was therefore ignored. The Report stated that the Council had 'delayed unreasonably in responding to tenants' complaints about John and in acting on their findings'.

The residents subsequently did receive an apology from the Council.

Whether the spread of permissive society standards is to blame, or some other deep-seated social change, I do not know, but there is no doubt that complaints about bad neighbours have escalated sharply in recent years.

There seems to have been a deliberate policy of putting problem families among quiet and law-abiding tenants in the optimistic belief that the good behaviour of the latter will have such an effect on the former that they will suddenly transform themselves into models of rectitude and responsibility.

It never works. What happens is that the lives of the good tenants are made a misery, and the bad ones go on just the same as before.

Your neighbour's neat hedge does not encourage you to cut your own — you tend instead to hurl beer cans, plastic containers, fish-and-chip papers and old sacking into the orderly lines of your neighbour's privet, and let yours go hang. Serves them right for showing you up!

Similarly, their quiet and polite conduct is as a red rag to a bull. Faced with it, you don't emulate it — you play loud music and use the filthiest swear words known to Billingsgate when you are asked (courteously) if you would mind turning down the volume after midnight.

You encourage your children to bounce balls for hours at a time against your neighbour's walls. If your teenage son has a motorbike (more than likely), you suggest he gets a few pals over with their machines and have a good old game revving up their engines, tearing up and down the street, or doing stunts with barrels and planks.

At varying lengths of time after all this mayhem takes place, petitions are got up, the local MP and Councillors are visited in their surgeries and the Housing Department is contacted.

Very extreme cases have been known, after months or even years of purgatory for all within shouting distance, to be evicted.

But where do they go? And what is the ultimate solution to the problem? Social Psychologists, City Planners or Welfare Workers may ultimately come up with one that works. So far they have failed.

But of this I am sure — unless we find a way to bring back the concept that happy and contented living can exist only in a society whose people act responsibly and care about the well-being of others, the future is bleak indeed.

CHAPTER NINE

Roving Commissions

MPs tend to travel a good deal. This may be as Members of Select Committees of the House, some of which send their Members abroad to investigate the way in which their special subjects (health, pensions, transport, employment, etc.) are dealt with by other countries. The Home Affairs Select Committee has been known to look at what goes on at the other end of the immigration business in the countries of origin; how permits are sifted; how airlines regulate the matter; distances people have to come to put their cases to local British officials; whether claimed relationships are genuine, and matters of that sort.

The Trade and Industry Committee has looked into information technology in Japan and the USA and inquired into trade with East Europe in Hungary, Romania, Bulgaria, East Germany, Poland and Czechoslovakia.

The Transport Committee went to the Far East to conduct an inquiry into the decline of the UK registered merchant fleet, and to Copenhagen to inquire into air traffic control safety.

The Defence Committee visited Belize to inquire into British forces there, and to Hong Kong, Brunei, Singapore and Nepal to make an inquiry into the Brigade of Ghurkas. And even the Agriculture Committee visited Seattle and New Zealand to look at land use and forestry. It is fair to add that the time spent in these countries is invariably absolutely crammed and although I did not take part in any of the journeys mentioned above, I would bet that the Members had very little time indeed for relaxation.

Winston Churchill was one of the founding fathers of the Council of Europe, just after the War; and Britain (with all other member states of The Council of Europe and The Western European Union) must be represented at meetings of both those bodies. A politically-balanced delegation is drawn up to take on the task. Members will be appointed to serve on both these Parliamentary Assemblies for several years concurrently. I was assigned to these duties for 11 long years. The itinerary looks inviting: Paris about once a month, Strasbourg three or four times a year, Rome, Milan, Madrid, Madeira, Brussels, The Hague, Istanbul, Lisbon, Bonn, Athens, Oslo, Berlin, Malta, and sometimes even further afield to places like Hong Kong and China.

But having to leave home so often straight after (or even before) Sunday lunch, and the constant treks to airports, to say nothing of encountering hazards such as fog, strikes, misdirections and currency problems, is not funny. The huge backlog of mail which greets one's return, plus the irritating knowledge that one is going to have to miss debates in the House in which one was particularly anxious to speak, takes much of the gilt off the gingerbread.

There are other drawbacks. There is a pettiness about much of the work there. One can slave away writing a report, researching a subject, burning midnight oil; one can worry over it, struggle to clothe the relevant ideas in the right words, and then find that the Committee which has to pass it will argue heatedly for *hours* over the most trivial alterations in the wording: 'but' instead of 'and'; 'cover' instead of 'include'; 'share' instead of 'share out' ... and so on and so boringly on. And when it is all done, finally through the Committee and even through the Assembly itself, nothing very much ever seems to happen because of it. No changes, earth-shattering or otherwise, come about.

However, these two European Assemblies were not initiated to legislate, but to pool ideas and to establish contacts (and even friendships) between individual Parliamentarians, and they do that perfectly adequately. The Western European

Union is, to my mind, the more effective of the two. It deals with defence, and indeed is the *only* European Assembly with that competency. It explores, informs, and recommends (occasionally very technically) on defence matters, and Delegations hear Defence and Foreign Ministers from member countries with great regularity.

This can be interesting, but it can be extremely frustrating because any leading Minister from any of the member countries can take it into his head to come and speak to the Assembly, make that arrangement, turn up an hour late, and throw the whole programme into chaos. While I was for four years a member of the Presidential Committee, I tried very hard to bring in regulations which would limit the number of Ministers to four in a four-day session. My European colleagues reacted to my suggestions with strong disagreement — surely everyone (especially the press) wanted to hear Ministers, at any time Ministers might be gracious enough to seek occasion to utter? No go, Jill! So I tried instead to ensure that timetables were kept to. This, I am sorry to say, turns out to be a notion entirely foreign to most Europeans. At Westminster, the heavens can fall or the earth come to an end: Madam Speaker will still enter the Chamber at 2:30 p.m. precisely on every normal sitting day (10 a.m. on a Wednesday, 9:30 a.m. if it is a Friday). If a session at Strasbourg or Paris is timed to begin at 10:00 a.m., it *might* actually start then. On the other hand, no one might be there until 10:10, or even sometimes 10:15. Committee meetings are notorious in this regard, and rarely seem to start less than 25 minutes late. Of course, the inevitable result of this is that things get more and more out of hand, week by week. People start to turn up late because they feel confident that the meeting won't begin at the scheduled time. At least 10 or 15 minutes seem to be wasted at the start of almost every session, while the punctual few hang around waiting for the rest to put in an appearance. This used to infuriate me, but I could do absolutely nothing about it.

But the occasional irritation is more than balanced by the sheer pleasure and fascination involved in learning about

Europe and the Europeans — especially during those times when one has been called upon to write a report on a particular topic. This provides a marvellous excuse for research into the varying customs of the Basque, the Tuscan, the Walloon and the Dane — even the odd Icelander — as they relate to the subject-matter of the report.

I can remember doing one report about prisons and the different European penal systems — a very interesting assignment. I visited prisons in different countries and read reports from many others. My hackles were raised, though, at the amendments which my colleagues tabled to my carefully-researched report, at the point where it was to be debated by the Assembly. One amendment wanted all prisoners, anywhere in Europe, to have any textbooks, on any subjects, whatever the cost, made available to them on demand. Another advocated that every prisoner leaving a prison should be guaranteed a job by their government. I countered these lofty notions with some heat, telling my disapproving European colleagues that they had hearts as big as buckets and brains as big as peas. At the time, unemployment was rife throughout Europe, and I failed to see how any of the national governments would be in a position to guarantee a job to a convict who had done his time — and even if they could, it was grossly unfair to law-abiding citizens, who had access to no such guarantee. I could foresee people breaking plate-glass windows to go to prison, so that they would get a job.

Not that my words made a ha'pennyworth of difference — these amendments, and others like them, were solemnly passed. I comforted myself with the certain knowledge that nothing would actually *happen* — which, of course, it didn't.

I did enjoy a lot of my time in Europe, though. There was almost always time to explore after the meetings were over, and some of the friends I made at that time still come and stay in my home in England.

Without question, the biggest drawback to serving as a delegate to the Council of Europe and the Western European Union is being out of sight and out of mind at Westminster. The parliamentary career goes on hold, and hope of exerting a beneficent influence is quite unfulfilled. Let new Members, aspiring to office, take note: you will never impress the Whips, the Ministers, your Leader or your colleagues by going off to Europe. As far as they are concerned, you are missing, believed 'paired'.

Europe has waxed in importance in all our minds, in the last generation, and we place a great deal of our hopes in it: but the older Commonwealth ties still count for something, and as MPs we have the Commonwealth Parliamentary Association, to remind us of them.

The Commonwealth Parliamentary Association, UK Branch, is run by an elected Committee of MPs, aided by a competent secretariat. They hold an annual conference every Autumn, and all Commonwealth countries which can host that conference take turns to do so. I once went to a CPA annual conference in Australia, on which we had a high old time. Our Australian hosts transported us for extensive trips round their country, prior to the opening of the conference, and we got to know each other and the Australian way of life at the same time. This was in 1970, and one message that came across loud and clear was the concern of Australian farmers over a catastrophic fall in the price of wool. As more and more synthetic fibres took over the market, Queensland sheep farmers, once prosperous men, were paying off their 'hands' and living solely on the produce of their vegetable gardens. I do not know how many went broke nor how long it was before consumers found out that synthetic fibres were nowhere near as good as wool, but it happened, and the last time I inquired about the Australian wool trade, the prices were encouraging, the forecasts optimistic and a record amount of wool had been processed in Australia.

Itinerant MPs soon learn the hard way not to go to far-away places in one long flight, for duties are scheduled to begin the moment one leaves the plane, and, after some 28 or 30 hours incarcerated aloft, stomachs, as well as time-clocks, become thoroughly disorientated. One is in no fit state to be taken from the airport to meet the welcoming committee and begin the first meeting.

So, *en route* to the Antipodes, I had decided to make two stop-overs: one in India to see the Taj Mahal, and one in Bangkok to see the Floating Market. I hasten to interpolate that one does, of course, pay for this kind of pleasant diversion out of one's own pocket. Let the taxpayer relax.

At New Delhi I waited, sitting on a hard seat, for the small plane to Agra. But a monsoon was raging and passengers were informed that there would be a delay of at least three hours before take-off. I looked around for some congenial company and got into conversation with two American women. They were not travelling together, but they had teamed up to endure the wait. I suggested we all go and get a drink in the airport café. There was, of course, no alcohol sold there. However, the older of the two women carried a hip flask, and we all had a generous slug of gin in our lemonade. As we talked, the flask-owner suddenly held up her hand. 'Oh! Do just look at that cute little chipmunk', she cooed. We peered around obediently, then froze with horror. Her 'chipmunk' was a large rat, running around the tables energetically, pausing only to eat various food scraps in its path. Our yells brought a covey of embarrassed but active turbanned kitchen staff, who killed the rat almost at our feet.

Which all goes to show that short-sightedness can be a blessing. She thought she saw a chipmunk and was not in the least perturbed. We knew we saw a rat, and were petrified.

Having arrived in Agra, we did all the right things, like seeing the Taj first by moonlight, and then at intervals throughout the day. I am told that visitors who go there today cannot see this moonlit vision because of some security problem. This is a shame.

Other wonders of the world can be disappointing — Niagara Falls seen from the American side is tame; the Pyramids are not

lonely and remote but teeming with people, camels and
screaming kids; the Hanging Gardens of Babylon and the
Colossus of Rhodes haven't even been in existence for
centuries — but the Taj Mahal is the wonder of all wonders.

White marble, and glistening with semi-precious stones, the
architecture is absolutely brilliant. It was completed in 1653,
having taken a team of 20,000 men 21 years to build.
Perspective is gauged so cleverly that the letters spelling out
words from the Koran at the summit of the huge arches appear
to be exactly the same size as the words at the bottom. The
towers are constructed at a slight tilt, leaning away from the
tomb, so that, should an earthquake occur, they would fall
away from the building and not on it. But you can see no sign of
the tilt with the naked eye.

The Taj Mahal looks quite different when one views it at
different times in the day. By moonlight, it is a gleaming,
shimmering, white palace from a fairy-tale. When the sun starts
to rise, it mirrors the green, green lawns around the palace, and
becomes a place of Neptune, or of forest dryads. At noon it is so
blindingly bright that one can hardly bear to look at it. Later,
with the sun moving down in the sky and striking the Red Fort
across the Yamuna River, the Fort is reflected too and the Taj is
pink against the green grass and the water.

Its beauty is tinged with the old, tragic story of the Mughal
Emperor, Shah Jahan, who built it to be an everlasting memorial
to the love he bore for his wife Mumtaz Mahal. She died in
childbirth, and few women throughout history have had such a
lasting tribute of devotion. The tiny intricate flowers on her
tomb are of inlaid jasper, agate, opal, carnelian, lapis lazuli and
blood stone. The masons have worked the coloured stones in
the marble, like embroiderers weaving coloured silks in a
tapestry. There are 35 different varieties of carnelian in a single
carnation leaf.

Outside the hotel where I stayed in Agra was a tree which,
from my window, I thought was covered in wonderful green and
yellow flowers. As I watched, entranced, there was a sudden
noise and all my flowers flew away. They were parakeets.

All tourists do touristy things, and I was assured that a visit to the local shops was not to be missed. As a keen and devoted shopper, I needed no urging, and soon found myself in a remarkable building called the Marble Emporium. Magic! There were intricately carved marble screens; marble plates inlaid with flowers and patterns, in jasper, jade, turquoise and mother-of-pearl; table-lamps, candlesticks, figurines, animals, book-ends, even goblets and stools. A tall brown man in a spotless white suit was helpful.

My eye lighted on a most unusual specimen. Everyone knows about the three wise monkeys — hear no evil, speak no evil, see no evil; little paws over ears, mouth, eyes, and a lesson to us all. So no surprise, then, to see there, slightly hidden behind a large marble tray, a marble branch whereon sat a neat row of primates striking the usual poses. Only there were not three, but *four* of them. This intrigued me no end. I interrupted my polite salesman, who was in full flow by now. 'Excuse me, but could you explain about those marble monkeys over there?', I said. 'I've never heard of the *four* wise monkeys.'

He appeared not to hear. 'Memsahib must look at this beautiful coffee table. Would be a special price for Memsahib.' No, no, I did not want a coffee table, thanks all the same; but I really *would* like to know about the four monkeys. He tried again. 'This very lovely tray — look at the work in it', he cajoled.

I said I did not want a tray; I was determined to know about the monkeys. He shifted his feet. His collar seemed rather tight. A distinctly hunted look appeared in his eyes. This mad and obstinate English woman would not be silenced. He cleared his throat. 'W-e-l-l ... Memsahib must understand that we have a big problem in India. Too many babies come.'

I saw at once that the fourth monkey had his paws over his, er, reproductive organs, and a pained look on his little face.

Had the poor salesman been more matter-of-fact about it, I would have been matter-of-fact, too, but his acute embarrassment spread to me, and I hastily averted my eyes and bought a small table-lamp.

Back home, I told the story to Monty. 'What!' he said, 'you mean you didn't buy them?'

It took me *years* before I found the four monkeys again, and these were not marble, but bone. I bought them in a street market in Lahore. Monty was delighted, and they have remained a great talking-point with visitors ever since.

There is another incident which comes to mind and memory when I think of that time in Agra. At the side of the road back to the hotel sat a thin, bright-eyed man in a loincloth. In his hands he held a small, furry animal, and at his side was a wicker basket with a lid. He got to his feet as I passed. He explained that he had a cobra in the basket, and if I gave him two rupees he would let the snake out of the basket, and I would see the mongoose kill it. Little did he know that I would gladly have given him *four* rupees (or even 40) so long as he kept the cobra in the basket and out of my sight. As it was, I mumbled something and walked on rather quickly. Then I was puzzled. Surely a cobra was worth more than two rupees? Why not wait until he had gathered a more sizeable audience, *all* paying two rupees?

Later, at the High Commissioner's residence, I asked about this, and was told that, had I forked out, the man would certainly have let the snake out, but the trick was that the mongoose would have been fed very recently and have no desire for a meal. It would merely have played around with the snake, patting at it a bit, perhaps, but doing it no harm. The small-scale showman would have 'tried', but eventually, regretfully, put the snake back, with apologies to Memsahib. After all, he didn't want to have to go off and catch another one somewhere.

After India, still *en route* for Australia, I stopped over in Bangkok. The Floating Market is a well-known tourist attraction; but I was still fascinated to see people selling, haggling, and buying from the small, flat boats. There was every kind of food to be had — bananas, paw-paw, oranges, melons, meat, fish, and even charcoal. The customers stepped across from boat to boat, carrying their purchases in plastic bags, for all the world as if they were in Tesco's.

Many people seemed to live on the river Chaophya itself, in funny little wooden houses on stilts among the bamboo at the riverside. They came down their rickety steps to wash themselves and their clothes and their babies in the water, which is so filthy as to be totally opaque — a bit like thin mud, turgid and greenish. I watched one man even cleaning his teeth in it! I asked my boatman/guide about these ablutions, which seemed to me distinctly dodgy. He paused in his rowing to inform me that these people had built up a total immunity to the germs, bacteria and other hazards in the water. 'But', he said with relish, 'if you were to brush your teeth in it you'd be dead in twenty-four hours'. I did not doubt it.

On I went to Australia, and the 1970 CPA Conference duly began, in Parliament House, Canberra. The Governor-General opened the proceedings, and the first debate, on International Affairs and Defence, ranged over countries and issues as diverse as Laos and Cambodia, Malaysia, Singapore, Japan's economic success, the dispute between India and Pakistan, and the Soviet presence around Africa's coast. There was a call for the Americans to quit Vietnam, and a reference to the fact that this was the first Commonwealth Conference to take place without Rhodesia. A delegate from Ghana claimed it was 'crystal clear' that South Africa intended to annex Namibia — an accusation happily not borne out by subsequent events. A Canadian delegate declared humbly that Canada was not a great power, but then surprised us all by announcing that his country was seeking close links with China. Ceylon appealed to Australia for a relaxation of her immigration laws. 'Whites are allowed to settle in your country', accused the delegate, 'but not people of my colour.' Trinidad had a go at Britain over Rhodesia ... and Kenya, Malawi, Jamaica, Sierra Leone and

little St Vincent all promptly joined in the attack, for various
reasons, and at various lengths. Only Gibraltar had a good word
to say for us. I sometimes wonder if what really unites the
Commonwealth is a univeral dislike of the United Kingdom —
coupled, nonetheless, with a universal readiness to take
advantage of our Aid programmes.

The second debate was entitled 'The Parliamentarian', and,
so far as I could see, had been tabled so that new Parliaments
could be given a few tips — from representatives of 'old-hand'
Parliaments such as our own — as to how they should run
themselves. Knotty problems — such as to what extent an MP
must bow to his Party's directives, and what should be done to
him if he doesn't — were discussed; since some of the delegates
came from Parliaments which had only been going a year or
two, it would have contained a lot of useful meat for them.

A lady MP from Fiji brought us a charming vignette of what
must surely have been the most unsophisticated Parliament of
all those taking part in the Conference. 'We are one of the
smallest nations', she said, 'and certainly not wealthy. In the
whole of our Parliament we do not have even a pool typist. I
carry a triplicate book with carbons, and use it to write my
letters to Ministers and other people. Then I file the copies
somewhere. We have no amenities in our House at all. Well,
we have one Common Room where we have morning tea, but
we do not have desks or anything like that.'

The Ceylonese delegate was clearly horrified at this picture
of deprivation, but the lady shrugged off his pity with a
dignified statement that she was not complaining. 'We do not
have the means to pay, and we realise this. We are a patient
people, and we are prepared to do our best with what we have.
It is no use carping.' I gave her a cheer. I thought she
deserved it.

I did not approve nearly so much of the Kenyan delegate,
who talked a great deal about democracy, while at the same
time informing us that his was a one-party state. He thought
that what made his country democratic was that there could be
as many as five candidates for a Parliamentary seat, and the

people could choose, in an election, which of the five they wanted. The fact that they all held identical views and were all from the same political party did not count as undemocratic, in his judgement. Clearly cast in the Cromwellian mould, he announced impressively in his opening remarks that he had been elected because God wanted him to serve his people. There is no answer to that.

My own major duty at this Parliamentary Conference was to open the debate on Conservation and Pollution. I had worked very hard on this, having spent many hours researching the facts back in Westminster. Our Parliament had recently passed the Clean Air Act, and London was starting to have public buildings scrubbed clean of the grime of centuries, secure in the knowledge that, once clean, the buildings would remain so. But there was still the pollution menace of motor cars and transport lorries emitting poisonous carbon monoxide, and diesel fumes; there were the insecticides and nitrate fertilisers on farmers' field crops; there were industrial wastes and detergents flowing into rivers and canals; there was noise pollution, pollution by dumping, and the rate at which grassland was being paved and built on was a big worry. I even quoted the words of a currently-popular song: 'They paved Paradise, and put up a parking lot', I almost crooned. I was green as green, long before any of the Green Parties in Europe appeared on the scene. I discussed sewage and water supplies, causing audible revulsion when I informed my audience that if you drink a glass of tap water in London, you are likely to be the seventh person to have consumed it. I could feel, if not see, my entire audience make an instant resolution to stick to whisky when in the British capital. Moving on swiftly, I warned them that some baby foods contained over three times the permitted safe maximum daily dose of nitrate for an adult — though I added the caveat that this was only what 'the experts' had said, and experts (as I have earlier remarked) are notoriously inaccurate.

I mention all these things to indicate once more how very wide-ranging are the subjects MPs have to try and master in the course of their duties. One thing is for sure — no experienced MP is ever *unable* to join in any conversation, on any subject, at any time, at any dinner party or in any public bar — though, of course, he or she may *choose* not to take part. We are indeed Jacks of all trades, and masters of precious few.

CHAPTER TEN

Hurling Glasses Across Russia

L ARGER, and more all-embracing, than the Commonwealth
Parliamentary Association is the Inter-Parliamentary
Union, membership of which is open to countries all over the
world, provided they have a Parliament, or its equivalent. It was
founded in 1888 by two MPs – one British, one French – and
its objectives, unchanged over the years, are 'to promote
personal contacts between members of all Parliaments, and to
unite them in common action to secure and maintain the full
participation of their respective States in the establishment and
development of democratic institutions and the advancement
of the work of international peace and co-operation'. If the
objectives are unchanged, the membership is not: it steadily
increases. In 1967, 76 countries belonged; by 1994 there were
131, and the number is still rising.

There are two conferences a year which in effect constitute
an informal international Parliament, where MPs of all
countries and parties meet and freely discuss the problems of
the day. Apart from these, there are frequent interchanges of
visits by Members of Parliament from each country, providing a
valuable education for the MPs, and an insight into the
problems of their respective lands. The monitoring of elections
in newly-democratic countries is carried out, by the
Commonwealth Parliamentary Association in the Commonwealth countries, and solely by the IPU outside them. The
British-Irish group section of the IPU has had much work to do
as relations between our two countries have improved.

I became a member of the IPU executive and was elected as
the British Chairman in 1994, but my earliest experience of the
group was as a young member in 1967 when I was chosen to
join a delegation to Soviet Russia. Looking back now, it was

more of a privilege than we realised then, to be able to see at first hand the Russia of the Communist era, before *glasnost* and *perestroika*. We observed how the people lived and worked, and listened to their opinions. We heard about their customs, their laws and their history.

As IPU delegates and guests of Mother Russia, we were clearly on an altogether higher plane than mere tourists, receiving blatantly preferential treatment in hotels, restaurants, museums and theatres. We did not have to wait for meals, wait in queues, or endure the amount of petty bureaucracy that they did. We had special trains, buses and planes, while they seemed to be forever waiting for theirs to arrive. The contrast was stark and startling.

Prior to our departure we were briefed as to what to expect, how to behave, and what to wear. The British Ambassador of the day, Sir Geoffrey Harrison, had kindly come over to Britain to put us in the picture — even though we were due to meet him later in Moscow. One snippet he imparted to me was clearly quite hilarious, if one only knew why. 'There was a lady', he said, 'who once went to Irkutsk in *nylon* stockings!'

Waiting for my merry laugh at this poor woman's stupidity, all he got was a puzzled look. I asked, rather hesitantly, what was wrong about wearing nylon stockings in Irkutsk?

'Oh, just that the cold freezes them into your legs!', said he with ghoulish relish. 'The first few layers of skin peel right off with the stockings when you take them off!'. As we had just been told that we were going to Irkutsk, I quickly made a mental note to purchase some golf stockings. I never found out if he was telling the truth, for our visit was in May, and even Siberia does not freeze over in May.

Our programme was clearly going to be strenuous. First stop was Moscow, for meetings with the Russian equivalents of our Speaker and Lord Chancellor — in other words, the chairmen of the two chambers of the USSR Parliament. We would also attend several sessions of various Standing Committees, visit schools, hospitals, museums, factories and universities. Then we were headed eastward — about 3,300 miles across the Ural mountains into Siberia. We learned that the last frost in that area was usually in mid-July, and the first in mid-August, so our visit fell at quite a good time, when it would not be much colder than a January in England. But tours of Bratsk and Irkutsk, near the borders of Outer Mongolia, which we had scheduled after that, could still be distinctly chilly. Then we would trek back across West Siberia to Leningrad, and on south to Baku in Azerbaijan on the shores of the Caspian Sea, before returning to Moscow for final meetings.

I shall never forget that trip — so many lessons, so many impressions, so many surprises. The first shock was the enormous difference between people's status, in a country where I had been led to believe all were equal.

We travelled the wide Moscow streets in an impressive black Russian staff car. I noted with puzzlement that we swept majestically along in an unencumbered lane in the centre of the road, which was marked out with yellow lines. On each side were traffic jams of dismal-looking buses, beaten-up old vans, lorries with people inside and a few — a very few — private cars. Hire purchase was unknown and no one could normally expect to be able to buy a car of his own. The people in the buses and lorries stared at us in a lack-lustre way; not envious or resentful — just stolidly resigned.

'Why are we here in this empty traffic lane, while everyone else is stuck in those lanes?' I asked my accompanying KGB man. His name was quite unpronounceable and I called him 'Buster', which was the nearest I could get. He shot me a glance from his black eyes in which I detected contempt for those who asked stupid questions. 'Zis is ze VIP lane', he explained, as to an idiot child. 'Zey are not VIPs. Zey cannot come here.'

'I see', said I, pressing on. 'But who, exactly, *can* drive in this lane?' Buster gave a faint sigh. 'Here are ze high ranking Officers of ze Army, ze Navy and ze Air Force', he explained, 'Generals and above'. I reflected that there couldn't, surely, be many Generals and even less numbers above that rank, but he had not finished. 'Here also are ze Cosmonauts'. Pause. 'Ze ones who have been up.' Not many of *those*, I thought. 'Also, of course, here are ze politicians', said Buster.

'Well, Buster', I said, 'now I'll tell you something. If we had a special traffic lane down Whitehall and round Parliament Square for the politicians in my country, there would be a revolution'. There would be, too.

I found out later that there were two other groups who could use the magic lane — ambulances and fire engines. That seemed more reasonable, I thought.

It was undeniable at that time that if you were one of Russia's élite, you ate a great deal better than if you were a mere run-of-the-mill comrade. They gave us a most elaborate lunch at the Kremlin which had 16 courses; and indeed, all the official meals we ate on that trip were multi-coursed. At the Kremlin lunch, I had not yet learned the ropes. We were ushered into the ornate dining-room and shown to our seats, where we found, ranged to the right and left of every place-setting, a positive galaxy of knives, forks and spoons. One's nearest neighbour had to be about four feet away, to leave room for the cutlery. Also at each place were three glasses: one filled with Georgia water (like Perrier or fizzy Malvern Water), one filled with Georgia wine (which proved very good), and one, of course, with vodka.

The meal began. The first course was shark's fin soup. Covertly gazing at my lunch-neighbours (perish the thought that I should pick up the wrong spoon), I selected the right piece of cutlery and began to eat. Before we had had more than four spoonfuls of soup, a thickset man rose to his feet and held his vodka glass aloft. 'Ladies and Gentlemen', he boomed, 'now ve drink a toast to ze collective farm vorker.' We all stood up. We all raised our vodka glasses. 'The collective farm workers', we intoned. I took a small sip of my vodka and regained my seat.

The air was suddenly riven asunder by a stentorian monosyllable: 'YOU!!' I jumped, and glanced hastily to right and left, only to see everyone else staring back at me. What had I done?

'You have insult give!' he roared. 'You must *all* drink. *Finish* drink!.'

I rose to my feet, pink with embarrassment, and raised my glass again, all alone. 'To the collective farm workers!' I quavered — and drank the lot. As soon as every glass was put down on the table it was immediately refilled. I never saw so many wine waiters in my life.

Worse was to come. Even before the soup was finished another man got up and lifted his vodka glass 'to ze victorious Russian Army'. Out of the corner of my eye I could see the first man looking at me with a baleful glare. You just *dare* insult the Russian Army, he was clearly thinking. Not fancying the idea of a one-way ticket to the nearest gulag, I raised my glass high with everyone else, and tossed down the contents.

Having run the gamut of ze vunderful Russian women, ze marvellous Russian Army, ze brilliant Russian intelligentsia, ze brave Russian Cosmonauts, ze fabulous Russian dancers and ze amazing Russian scientists, I was beginning to fear I might behave in a very un-Parliamentary manner at any moment. Like sliding feet first under the table. To tell the truth, I do not normally have eight vodkas at lunch.

Then Heaven came to my aid. As the toast to the scientists concluded, I brought my glass down so sharply onto the table that it shattered into a million pieces. Calamity! It wasn't even just glass — it was cut crystal! I was numb with shock. 'Siberia here I come', I murmured to myself, wondering fleetingly if I would be able to plead diplomatic immunity.

But, amazingly, every man at the table rose to his feet to drink a toast to ME. I was the only one who knew what to do with a glass when she had finished with it! After that, I smashed my way cheerfully through the Soviet Union, flinging glasses to right and left with gay abandon. Now you know what to do if you are pressed to take more vodka than you can decently handle, during a Russian trip.

Occasions like this made me long to be able to write a proper letter home to Monty — he would have had such a good chuckle. However, there was a strict ban on letter-writing; by some strange quirk, the Soviet postal system apparently found letters quite beyond its administrative abilities. Postcards, on the other hand, seemed to present no such problems. Indeed, the authorities very kindly promised to give us as many postcards as we wanted — and they would even stamp them for us! This was an offer far too good to refuse; the certain knowledge that our words would be read and digested before we ever left the Soviet Union was not permitted to deter us in the slightest, and the whole delegation set about writing cards home, with great diligence and industry. Having given nearests and dearests unprecedented floods of cards, we turned our attention to friends and relatives, both close and distant. Anyone whose address we could recall was treated to the experience of getting a picture postcard of Moscow, Leningrad, Siberia or wherever we happened to be.

One of my colleagues, Lord Hankey, from 'the other place', showed me his final effort. Having exhausted his family, right down to second cousins and aunts not seen since his public school days, he sent a card to his dog. It had some fearfully up-market kennel name, but was known in the family as 'Wuffles'. The card was different, I'll say that. 'Woof woof' it read, 'wag, woof, wag. Snottle. Argh. Bow wow.' It finished, touchingly, 'Love from Daddy.'

Several months later we happened to be at the same dinner party, back in London. 'I say, Jill, did all those postcards you sent from Russia get back to the people you sent them to?', said his Lordship. Yes, as far as I knew all of them did, said I. 'So did mine', he informed me, '— well, all except that one to Wuffles.' The thought of the code-breakers in the Kremlin, no doubt supplied with massive computers, and plied endlessly with black coffee and cigarettes, trying to unravel the true meaning of 'woof, wag' and the rest was pure joy.

I do not know how often, if at all, ordinary tourist visitors to the Soviet Union at that time were allowed to see the treasures of the Kremlin; they are, I must report, quite breathtaking. A fantastic treasure of diamonds, rubies, sapphires, emeralds and opals, all mined in Russia, sparkle under the stern gaze of an armed guard. The old Imperial State Jewels of the Tsars blaze magnificently. Along the front of one showcase was what I took to be a white stone necklace — about 18 inches long and composed of round beads, all the same large size and, frankly, just a bit boring. As they seemed to be somewhat out of place amidst all this glory, I asked about them. To my surprise, they turned out to be pearls; because they had not been worn, they had 'died'. I knew that pearls benefit from constant use and cherishing, but until then I did not know that they perish if unworn. So, girls, remember: If you've got 'em, flaunt 'em — you'll save them for posterity and your heirs.

I was interested in visiting hospitals, and particularly keen to see to what extent the Soviets carried out the kind of advanced, high-tech operations then becoming fairly common in Britain. On my expressing this interest, it was immediately arranged for me to go and see a man who had had open-heart surgery that very morning. I was greatly concerned for him, though, since the media circus (which followed us everywhere) trooped in to his small ward after me. Reporters, cameramen and a TV crew crowded around his bed. I was as quick as possible, but I never heard how well the poor man survived the positive army of outside germs we must have brought in with us.

As to my verdict on Soviet medical care: well, the surgeons were, I have no doubt, highly skilled and the hospital a good and effective one; but it was the little things, like all doctors' white coats being un-ironed, and what seemed a surprising disregard for the normal standards of hospital hygiene, which bothered me.

More and more, I was mystified at the extraordinary compliance of the Soviet man in the street. How on earth had a whole people — a people with brains, courage and ingenuity, a people with many proud centuries of history — been content to

live for so long under a régime which denied them so much?
How could they allow themselves to be so bossed about by
bureaucrats — told where to live, how to behave, what to wear,
when to shop, where to shop? They were forever denied the
million little freedoms which the peoples of the West took for
granted; they had to queue endlessly for everything, and
endure shortage, rationing and abysmal quality, more than 20
years after the War had ended. Imagine being forced to live in
utterly dreary, monolithic flats, with every inch of floor space
calculated and allocated in strict ratio to the numbers in the
family! Or being refused all travel — even family picnics, let
alone holidays — except very rarely. Trips to foreign parts were
summarily disallowed by the authorities, with no reason ever
given. One would have thought that any intelligent people, well
aware of the wealth and power of their country, would have
staged a rebellion against a system which repressed and
controlled them to such a degree.

They were, even so, quite jolly folk. They admired our
clothes and possessions. One young girl, to whom I gave a small
bottle of perfume, was quite overwhelmed, her reaction out of
all proportion to the gift. So – they were not undesirous of
having such things for themselves, and they understood their
worth; and yet they obediently accepted the wretched,
constricted lifestyle that their Government decreed. It was to be
another 20 years before the reaction came about, before the
wind of change blew through the land. Why did it take so long?

I believe the answer may lie in the way the children were
brought up. When I asked if I might visit a child welfare clinic, I
was whisked off to what was, in fact, a crèche, divided into
sections, according to the age of the children. In the first room
were rows and rows of tiny babies, all wrapped up in small
identical tightly-swathed blankets. Then there were the
crawlers and the toddlers — all dressed exactly alike and each
doing what every other did. Next the two- and three-year-olds,
already completely obedient, marshalled in rows, playing,
eating and sleeping exactly as they were told.

'As the twig is bent so grows the tree', runs an old proverb.

Jill Knight, a Northampton Borough Councillor, meeting the Queen and Prince Philip, 1965.

The newly-elected Member of Parliament for Birmingham, Edgbaston in the city centre, 1966.

1995. Dame Jill Knight DBE MP with the Rt Hon John Major PC MP, Leader of the Conservative Party and Prime Minister since 1990.

Cavalier Cottage,
Stowe IX Churches,
Northants.

Before a Mr. Strachey started monkeying with nuts,
 Before a Shinwell-Gaitskell clique invented power-cuts,
When with bacon we were rasher and we all had bags of fuel,
In fact, through all the 20 years of Tory-ish misrule ;
Ah ! then the Festive season was a time of right good cheer,
 We all wished "A Merry Christmas" and "A Prosperous New Year,"
We both admit it's laughable to wish you these to date
 And yet we do—and hope Hard Labour ends in '48 !

from

Mr. and Mrs. Monty Knight,

left:
Monty's and Jill's
Christmas card, 1947.

below left:
Christmas card 1948:
labouring under a
bureaucratic régime.

below right:
1951, Christmas
pantomime written and
produced by Jill Knight.
Her characters include
Fairies Clementina,
Staffiloma, Skinwell and
Bevanda.

Oₙ Herbert Morrison's Service

Form S/21/129/4683C/T/L3/Help !
Ref. No.: Whistle.

Ministry of Pleasure Control,
"Stafford Grips,"
Taxpayer-By-The-Throat,
Andpocket.

Herewith permit to obtain one (1) Happy Christmas. This authorises you to purchase special Christmas ration of one (1) points free tin of snoek, and half share in one (1) holly berry.

Regulations Governing Issue of Permit :—

1. In order to avoid load shedding, and preserve National Health teeth, you are urged to postpone cooking your Christmas dinner until after May 1st.
2. You are ordered to be in bed by 10 p.m. to save light and fuel.
3. Please apply restrictive practices to Laughing, Joking, and Making Merry, as this uses up, energy better employed elsewhere.
4. There is a ban on singing, playing and dancing, as this may interfere with your neighbour's wireless.
5. There is a ban on listening to the wireless as this may interfere with your neighbour's singing, playing and dancing.

* * * *

Your application for a Happy New Year has not been granted, as there is to be no General Election before 1950.

* * * *

Nevertheless, we wish you RIGHT good cheer.

MR. & MRS. MONTY KNIGHT.

Cavalier Cottage,
 Stowe-IX-Churches,
 Northants.

Northampton Young Conservatives

PRESENT

El Grand Christmas Pantomime :

"The House that Jack Built"

Written and Produced
By
JILL KNIGHT

At Whitworth Road Club,

ON

Thursday, January 11th, 1951

At 7.30 p.m.

PROCEEDS IN AID OF YOUNG CONSERVATIVES
AND ELECTION FIGHTING FUNDS

PROGRAMME 2/6

J. STEVENSON HOLT LTD , NEWLAND NORTHAMPTON.

© BIRMINGHAM POST & MAIL

Campaigning in a vintage car, Birmingham 1966.

Parliamentary General Election, 1959
NORTHAMPTON BOROUGH

VOTE FOR
COUNCILLOR MRS.
JILL KNIGHT
CONSERVATIVE CANDIDATE

1959 General Election handbill.

Keeping in touch with local industry.

| Monty | Andrew | Jill | Roger |

Conservative women MPs with the Rt Hon Edward Heath PC MP, Leader of the Party, 1965-1975 and Prime Minister 1970-1974. Jill Knight is next to Mr Heath. Margaret Thatcher is 2nd from the right.

With Lord and Lady Home of the Hirsel. As the Rt Hon Sir Alec Douglas-Home PC MP, Prime Minister 1963-1964.

With the Rt Hon Selwyn Lloyd PC MP, Chancellor of the Exchequer, at the Conservative Party Conference, Scarborough 1960.

Officers of the 1922 Committee with the Rt Hon Margaret Thatcher PC MP, Leader of the Party 1975-1990 and Prime Minister 1979-1990.
l to r: Marcus Fox MP, Paul Bryan MP, Margaret Thatcher, Cranley Onslow MP, Jill Knight MP.

Margaret Thatcher and Jill Knight.

Fund-raising for a local charity.

Presenting school prizes.

ABOUT THE CONSTITUENCY

Tree-planting.

Opening a block of flats for the elderly.

Meeting the late King Faisal of Iraq, 1974.

An Audience with His Holiness Pope John Paul II, 1987.

WIDER
ROVING
COMMISSIONS

Inspecting an oil-drilling station in the USSR, 1967.

left: Receiving the Freedom of the City of San Francisco, 1970.

below: Meeting Afghan leaders in the Khyber Pass during the Russo-Afghan War, 1989.

Buckingham Palace,
MBE Investiture, 1964.

Buckingham Palace Investiture,
1985 Dame Commander of the Order of the British Empire.

These people had been trained from earliest childhood; they took in submission and conformity with their mothers' milk — and I am not sure they had too much of *that*, since every Soviet woman was expected to return to work when her child was two weeks old. She would take her baby to the crèche at 7:00 a.m., and pick it up at 7:00 p.m. I reflected that one could not exert much influence over one's child if one only had it when it had just woken up, and when it was sleepy and wanting its bed. The same pattern seemed to be followed later on, with the children being taken off to camp by the authorities in the school holidays. I should imagine the children were hard-pressed to remember what their parents looked like — and vice versa.

I tried to find out whether the children *had* to go to the crèche, and later to the camp. But I got no answer — my questions were always parried with 'Well, of course, *all* mothers *like* to have the burdens of looking after their children taken away — see how well the children look! All are fed and cared for, and the parents know they are safe and warm, and being looked after by trained people.' Then they'd usually go on to remark: 'You don't have such good arrangements made for mothers in your country, do you?'

In general, the Soviet people I met had some peculiar ideas about what we have. That presented another part of the answer to the puzzle of the blind acceptance of such poor standards. At that time (it was 1967), no outside TV reached the Soviet viewer, and they knew virtually nothing about the standard of living of their peers in other countries.

We were not allowed to accept hospitality from the ordinary people we met, but certain selected citizens were permitted (perhaps ordered?) to invite us to their homes. I went into one woman's flat, accompanied as usual by the local press corps. She showed me round her home with great pride. It was spartan but spotless. She led me into her tiny kitchen, and showed me the taps as if they were gold-plated, clearly expecting some reaction from me. I couldn't quite see what she expected me to say, but I nodded, smiling. 'Look', she said, 'I have a hot-water tap!' Well, yes, I could see that much. 'I don't have to heat the water; hot water comes from the tap', she persisted. 'Um', I said. 'But you don't have hot-water taps in *your* kitchen, do you?', she said. I didn't have the heart to put her right. She would not have believed me, anyway.

We worked hard on that trip. There were several talks given in the Kremlin for us, and visits arranged to a great number of factories. Naturally, while in Moscow, it was obligatory to go and see Lenin's tomb, too; a frightful place which appears to have been constructed from huge slabs of frozen liver. The dead Leader lies visible for all to see, as he has for all these years, since his death in 1924. He has his hands clasped across his chest and his eyes closed as if in sleep. I did not care to know the macabre details of exactly what arcane chemical substance preserves him thus.

Our delegation laid a wreath on the mass grave of the citizens of Leningrad (St Petersburg, as it is now, as originally, known) who perished in the 900-day German siege of the city, which began in 1941. Half a million died, many from starvation. At the time when we were due to place the wreath on the memorial, the rain was coming down in a steady and remorseless torrent, and we had to walk, at a funereal pace, from the wrought-iron gate to the tomb, which seemed like a distance of about a mile. The rain poured down: we got wetter and wetter. My hair was sodden and hanging over my face like rats' tails. Still we held the wreath solemnly aloft, our pace never quickening, our dignity never slipping. Parliament should have been proud of us.

In Baku, on the Caspian Sea, we learned all about the oil resources of that area. Surrounding the town, and clothing the hills as far as the eye could see in all directions, were hundreds and hundreds of oil derricks. We went on one of these, clambering around in the hot sun and viewing the ones built out (up to 28 miles out!) into the sea itself. The only thing they did not tell us was the worth of the revenue the oil brought in.

Siberia was impressive. They welcomed us with bunches of roses, which in any other place would have been delightful but not particularly unusual. To grow roses in that climate, however, with snow on the ground for 10 months of the year, is next to impossible. Still, they had learned a trick or two about fertilisers, use of glass, and some very accurate timing: and a guest gets roses, and feels honoured and humbled, all at once.

During a tour of the massive Shelekhovsky aluminium combine in Irkutsk I asked (slightly tongue-in-cheek) how on earth they persuaded men and women to come and work in such conditions. It was not only a question of the perpetual and marrow-chilling cold: the processes involved in the production of aluminium are themselves far from healthy to humans. I still do not know whether to believe the answer I got: that the earnings there were much higher, the hours of work much shorter, and that there was free milk, butter and cream. This may well be so; but I suspect the workers never went anywhere else, and I do not think they invariably went there of their own free-will; although certainly some were born there and knew very little about Moscow life. Holidays were sometimes possible, I was told, and the resorts on the Black Sea were very popular.

There is a most beautiful lake not far away from the complex, which we were taken to see. We rode on a boat which bounded across the water in a most exhilarating fashion, and allowed us precious glimpses of the charming white seals which live there. The lake is called Lake Baikal, and in the brief time when the water and the surrounding woods are not in the grip of winter, it is one of the loveliest places one could imagine.

We went to a fur-processing works near Bratsk. The women who showed us round displayed the finest ermine with the comment: 'In the days of the Tsars, only the so-called noble people were allowed to wear ermine. Now everyone is allowed to wear ermine.' I have to say that in the whole length and breadth of our extensive travels in the Soviet Union I saw not one single person wearing it. Other furs, yes: ermine, never.

An interesting story emerged as we were being shown round this fur-processing factory. A small animal with highly sought-after fur, such as a mink, always had to be shot through the eyes, since trapping or less careful shooting would ruin the pelt. This created a demand for some pretty extraordinary sharp-shooting. During the Second World War, such expert shots were hastily recruited into the Russian Army, and were used with such phenomenal success against the Germans that they, the Germans, became convinced that the Russians had some new and highly secret supergun. They expended a good deal of expensive effort researching into the mythical dreaded weapon — meeting, naturally, nothing but total frustration, since it never existed. The magical weapon was, in fact, ordinary human skill — but honed to an extraordinary degree.

There is a five-hour time change between Eastern Siberia and Moscow. We were due to leave at 12 noon. Our hosts, whose kindness and hospitality had been absolutely unstinting throughout, gave us a magnificent brunch: 10 courses, with caviar, vodka, the lot. Many toasts were drunk, and ditto some of the guests. I did my smashed-glass routine, which had become second nature by now, and was a sure-fire success. As it came round to time for us to catch the plane, more roses were produced. There were hugs and kisses all round, thanks on all sides and cries of 'Come again!' from theirs.

Another benefit conferred by the Supreme Soviet on their guests was to be able to ride in a huge black car right up to the steps of the plane. None of the usual airport travail — booking in, checking luggage, and walking for miles through endless corridors to the gate. It did help to alleviate the pangs of regret I had felt at *not* having a chance to travel on the Trans-Siberian Railway.

Anyhow, feeling somewhat over-fed after that gargantuan brunch, we dragged ourselves up the steps and into the aircraft. We settled into our seats and fastened our seat-belts, all hoping for nothing more than a good post-prandial nap. The flight began. Half an hour passed, and the time was 12 o'clock (again). Along came the air hostess with lunch. Now I do not know whether Aeroflot has changed its policy since those days, but Russian air hostesses then were incredibly large and amazingly ugly. This woman, who could have doubled for a Sherman tank, and possessed similar levels of charm and subtlety, poked a laden plastic tray at me. 'Niet, bajalst', I demurred, trying out my Russian. She glared at me, outraged. 'You', she said, 'It'. It was only too clear she meant 'eat', and even clearer that I was going to have to. You don't argue with a Sherman tank. I ate.

As the plane flew on, the clock, as far as we were concerned, was going backwards. Just over an hour went by, and we landed at Omsk. It was now 12:30 p.m. and, the dear Lord save us, there on the tarmac was the local Supreme Soviet, drawn up with military precision and little flags of friendship, all ready to take us to lunch. There was nothing for it — protocol says that when celebratory welcoming lunches have been prepared for guests, the guests have to eat them. England expected, and England was not betrayed, though three lunches in one day taxes the most dutiful stomach somewhat above and beyond the call of duty, and I am not sure I would do it again, even for the glory of the homeland. Still, we all survived.

Looking at the Russian Federation in the mid-1990s, it is difficult to see how the enormous changes that Gorbachev, Yeltsin and the mass of the Soviet people desire can actually be made to come about. It is one thing to acknowledge that Russia must move to a market economy, give freedom to its peoples, and operate as other industrial nations do. It is quite another to figure out where they should start.

The country has, as I write, a vast budget deficit and no debt markets to finance it. The State prints money to bridge the gap, while the Gross Domestic Product is low and falling. The black market is flourishing — one observer comments that while the official exchange rate is one rouble to the pound sterling, the black market rate is 40 or 50 roubles. Steep price rises are announced as a part of Government policy, and clearly very serious inflation is going to be inevitable.

The sheer scale of the changes they need to make is frightening. An economy based on total planning must be replaced by one built on the operation of market forces. Somehow a true, free, housing market will have to be engendered, and a labour market actually function, to provide willing labour where it is needed. Conventional wisdom has it so, certainly. But how do you develop a housing market, starting with a country where no one could originally own land, and where all city people live in flats owned by the State? Where will those city people ever find the money to buy their flats, anyway, let alone the shares that are now on offer by State enterprises anxious to change themselves into joint-stock companies?

Yet, if the size and number of the problems are daunting, the new Russia has two invaluable assets. The first is a nationwide determination to end the Communist system which has denied their people so much; and the second is the goodwill of the free world which, after all, has a strong vested interest in ending the fear and threat of Communist aggression.

It will take time, it will take huge chunks of international aid, and a totally new constitution in Russia; but it will succeed.

CHAPTER ELEVEN

Back-Benchers' Bills

IT is a moment of particular satisfaction in one's Parliamentary life when one introduces a Bill of one's own, and is able to see it progress through the mill of all the procedures which our unwritten constitution requires, and emerge into the light of day, eventually, as part of the law of the land.

Only a few months after I entered Parliament in 1966, a young Liberal MP named David Steel introduced a Private Member's Bill, which was to have a profound effect on my life. Entitled 'The Medical Termination of Pregnancy Bill', it was one of the most far-reaching Bills ever to be introduced by a Private Member. The Wilson Government, for its own reasons, gave it active support and extra Parliamentary time, without which it would certainly never have been passed. In all the years since then, there has hardly ever been one Parliamentary Session when opposition to the effects of the Abortion Act has not re-surfaced – either in the form of mammoth petitions or of attempts by back-bench Members to amend it. No Bill I can remember has ever aroused such strong feelings, and this is not to be wondered at; there can hardly be a subject which touches as fundamentally on standards of morals, of ethics and beliefs, as does abortion. It deals, after all, with life and death.

We knew that the subject would come up. During the 1966 General Election there had been extremely active campaigning by the Abortion Law Reform Association. Parliamentary candidates are at their most vulnerable when an Election is looming – they want as many votes as possible, and occasionally (foolishly) they give pledges of support to measures they simply haven't had the time to study. Fighting an election is a battle which takes every scrap of time and every ounce of

105

energy, for the three weeks or so that the campaign lasts — there really is no space for calm deliberation. At the time when this particular Election was going on, there was no organisation lobbying on behalf of the unborn, and so the pro-abortionists had the field to themselves. Their case had strong appeal, stressing the evils of back-street abortions, and the agonies of girls pregnant with an unwanted (and usually illegitimate) child.

When I received a form from the abortion lobby, asking for my support for their proposals, I had little except gut instinct to guide me. I said that I considered abortion justified for pregnancy occurring after rape, or if the mother's life was in danger: views I hold to this day. In such cases, abortion was already legal anyway. But I hesitated to go further, and I did make it amply clear that I was against abortion on demand. This was not, however, a subject I had studied deeply, and I was not too sure what effect Mr Steel's proposed changes might have if enacted. After the Election I had more time to think, and I was also cornered by two of the most eminent Consultants in Birmingham — one a psychiatrist and the other a gynaecologist — and told some very brutal facts about abortion. I began, then, to believe deeply that what Parliament was being asked to enact was wrong.

The arguments for easy abortion *sounded* plausible enough. 'Every child a wanted child', said the pro-abortionist — a pleasant and cosy sort of belief. But, said my psychiatrist visitor, many times a woman who is very worried about having become pregnant changes her feelings later on in the pregnancy, or shortly after the birth. The gynaecologist here took up the tale, telling me that for every mother who has a chance to get to know her child and *still* feels unable or disinclined to cope with bringing it up, there are thousands of infertile couples who long for a child to adopt. He saw such couples regularly in the course of his work, and felt constantly sad and frustrated that there were so few healthy, normal babies available for adoption. Surely we should not reduce the supply even further?

In the event, of course, the Act was passed, and we can see its effects. One of these is that the hard-pressed National Health Service has to spend millions on aborting unwanted (yet healthy) babies, while spending millions more on trying to create pregnancies in another set of women, using the latest scientific techniques to overcome Nature's limitations. An odd way to proceed.

Back in 1966, as I considered this proposed new law, it troubled me that if it became legal to kill a child (even a very tiny one) *solely because it was not wanted*, then how would we stop such reasoning from being carried further in the future? It could apply so easily to other human lives, particularly the very old, or the handicapped. Undoubtedly, the burdens of looking after a handicapped child are very great and should never be under-estimated; but surely a caring society should help the parents to cope, rather than get rid of the child?

On the horrors of back-street abortions, the lobbyists and campaigners were expansive and insistent. And the techniques certainly were quite ghastly — girls often died in agony at the hands of unqualified quacks; and well-meaning MPs, like everyone else, found the whole thing utterly repulsive. But some of the methods used, even by legitimate doctors, to abort babies (now as when the Abortion Act first became law) literally mean that the tiny bodies are torn limb from limb, with an arm coming first, then perhaps a leg, before the head and other pieces are pulled out. *That* is repulsive too, and since research has now confirmed that an unborn child does indeed feel pain, the cruelty is too appalling to contemplate.

It seems to me that the sensible way to deal with the problem of unwanted pregnancies should be birth control, rather than abortion. The one and only time I visited a private Abortion Nursing Home, I asked the same question of every one of the 32 women who were patients: 'What form of birth control were you using around the time when you became pregnant?' *Not one* had been using *any* form of birth control. It just was not something they did — ever. Yet contraceptives had never been so effective, and knowledge of the subject never so wide. Ah well, taking precautions means taking trouble, counting days or interfering with the passion of the moment. Besides, a girl might very well not get pregnant, if she has luck on her side — some get away with it for years! With the abortion option there for her if she does, why make a big fuss about it?

I could see this kind of attitude already becoming prevalent, even before the Act, and I was sickened by the irresponsibility of it. I became one of the strongest opponents of David Steel's Bill. Sadly, however, there were too few of us trying to defend unborn babies, against the tide of opinion pressing for 'a woman's right to choose', in this and every area. The child had no such rights, apparently.

When the Second Reading of the Bill took place, the Abortion Law Reform Association got its due reward for all that hard lobbying. An overwhelming majority of MPs had committed themselves by then to supporting the new measure, and duly did so, while only a tiny number spoke against it. The Bill consequently received a huge vote of support in the House, and was on its way.

After Second Reading, Bills must go into Committee, where every line, every subsection and every clause is scrutinised and can theoretically be amended or deleted in debate. The aim is to tidy and tighten the Bill, not to destroy its basic intention, and for this reason the Committees which study these Bills are made up in direct ratio to the numbers voting for and against the Bill at Second Reading. There were so few anti-abortionists on the Committee, because of this, that we never stood a chance — our influence was negligible. We tried hard: indeed, we deliberately sought to debate at such length that the Bill would run out of time. Private Members' Bills have normally only limited time, and delaying techniques can often work quite well. Unfortunately for us, and fortunately for Mr Steel, his Bill was strongly backed by the Labour Government.

We knew we were beaten when Ministers made it clear that they would ensure its passage, come time, go time.

Finally, in the Spring of 1967, the Abortion Act was on the Statute Book, and the law on the subject remained in exactly the same form until the passage of the Human Fertilisation and Embryology Bill in 1990, when the original protection given to an unborn child by the Infant Life Preservation Act — preventing its abortion after the 24th week — was abolished.

Many if not most of the pledges, promises and predictions we were given in 1966 by the pro-abortionists, about how the Act would operate, turned out to be false. We were told it would certainly not lead to abortion on demand — exactly what we now have. We were assured there would be no question of using aborted foetuses for experimentation — but this is now commonplace. We were promised, amazingly, that it would *not* lead to increased abortion — the figures have in fact soared, from an estimated 34,600 per annum up to about 180,000. How many of these abortions are really justified no one will ever be able to say, but we have taught our people irresponsibility in a field where responsibility is of paramount importance, and the implications are deep, wide, and serious.

It is generally assumed that back-bench MPs have little power, yet David Steel's Abortion Act must count as one of the most significant pieces of legislation ever passed. It has already led to the destruction of some two million lives.

Mr Steel got his Bill by winning a place in the annual ballot for Private Members' Bills. The procedure, briefly, is this: the ballot, which is actually a draw (as in a raffle), takes place at the start of the Parliamentary Session. Virtually all back-benchers put their names down. The first eight or 10 names drawn have a chance to get their measure right through and on to the Statute Book, but even for them the chance is quite small. Any Bill which is contentious will almost certainly be 'talked out', in Committee or on the floor of the House; and it can be hard to draw up a Bill that is both needed and uncontroversial.

There is also another small window of opportunity, allowing the back-bench MP to promote the legislation of his choice. On certain days — around 50 in the Parliamentary year — 10 minutes are set aside after Question Time, and before the start of the normal business of the day, in which a Member can make his or her case to the whole House that a certain Bill be enacted. Notice of this will go on the Order Paper, and it is open to any MP who dislikes the proposed measure to speak against it. Where that happens, a vote is taken. The new Bill, if given the approval of the House, can go forward as a normal Bill; however popular it might be, such a Bill rarely becomes law. Procedural boulders will be strewn in its path. Specifically, it will have very, very little Parliamentary time, and a Private Member's Bill needs time like a plant needs sunlight. Every detail of it must be weighed and tested in debate, through Second Reading, into the Committee stage and Report, and on through Third Reading; and after that it must go through similar hurdles in the Lords. It must complete all stages of the process before the end of the Parliamentary year, else it tumbles into limbo. The first requirement for success, then, is that such a Bill must be very short and very simple, with no ambiguous or controversial words or clauses that might give an opportunity for would-be wreckers to filibuster.

I claim some expertise in the navigation of Ten-Minute Rule Bills through the horrors and hazards of our unique British legislative system: five of my own measures have reached the Statute Book via, or partly via, this route.

The first was only a year or so after I entered Parliament. I had visited a factory in Birmingham's jewellery quarter, at the request of the constituent whose firm it was. Although this firm did not work with gold and precious stones, they produced high-quality jewellery of silver, set with semi-precious stones of every hue and shade. I was shown the whole process of design and manufacture, and finally taken to the board room, where the Managing Director opened a large safe and drew out tray after tray of what I thought were two identical brooches, two identical rings, two identical bracelets, pendants and so on. When I asked why he was showing me these things, the purpose of the invitation became clear. 'This one's mine, and that one is made by a competitor', said he, repeating the words again and again as he pointed to the different pieces. He said he was sick and tired of keeping a highly-paid staff to design jewellery, and sending salesmen around the country and the world getting orders, only to lose those orders when inferior copies appeared, even before his high-quality ones had had a chance to sell in the shops. It turned out that within 24 hours of his merchandise appearing on the market a piece would be bought and flown out to somewhere like Hong Kong where, using the lost-wax process or a similar one, cheap copies would be turned out for a mass market. 'What are you going to do about it?' he asked. This racket, which was costing his business serious money, was perfectly legal. Clearly, it should not be!

So what *was* I going to do about it? I could have written to the Secretary of State, put down a Parliamentary Question, raised the matter in an Adjournment Debate, or applied to take representatives of the jewellery trade to the Minister. I considered and rejected all these, and went instead for a Ten-Minute Rule Bill, believing that a direct approach to a straightforward problem would be the best one.

It was early in the Session. This meant that a Bill was less likely to run out of time, but also that there would be hot competition for a slot. To get one, you have to be at the head of a queue on a given morning, at the door of the Public Bill office tucked away on one of the upstairs corridors of the Palace of Westminster. The only sure way to be first was to arm yourself with a sleeping bag, a flask and a sandwich or two, and spend a thoroughly uncomfortable night sleeping on the threshold, like a medieval knight protecting his liege lord. This is a custom which has not survived the pressure to make the running of the House easier for Members. Nowadays getting to the door by 7:30 a.m. is usually sufficient, though one must still camp out there until 10:00 a.m., when the Clerk commences work.

I had certainly tackled a tricky subject for my first Bill, even though the essential problem was quite simple. Copyright laws were, I found, a jungle. Every book, article, poem or song was protected by copyright as soon as it was written, and there were laws allowing inventors to patent any invention which had moving parts, but for *design*, there was neither copyright nor patent. It was a fairly gigantic loophole — anyone could copy and use drawings which resulted in an immobile object. Or, indeed, they could copy the object itself, with very convincing results, as I had seen.

To keep my Bill short and simple was essential, but difficult. With drafting help I did it, and, with something of a fair wind generated by many in industry who had clamoured for such legislation for years, it passed through all its stages and became law.

Its simplicity meant that there were hardly any exemption clauses, and it protected design of just about everything from fireplaces to cutlery, wallpaper to furniture, ocarinas to alabaster owls. It had not been on the Statute Book for more than six months before one producer of jersey-knits successfully sued the mighty C & A over the copying of a fabric design, and shortly afterwards, a toymaker used my Act to get judgement against a plagiarist, thus preserving both his own livelihood and the quality of the product.

Four other measures which I introduced initially as Private Members' Bills reached the Statute Book through the infallible method of being taken over by the Government of the day.

The first of these arose from a huge pile of evidence I received, to the effect that small children were being regularly poisoned through eating their parents' or grandparents' pills. Not all died, but all had to suffer the extremely unpleasant business of having their stomachs pumped empty, and many were very ill. Pills looked like sweets, and were sometimes left within easy reach of a toddler. Mothers might well keep their pill bottles sensibly on high shelves, but the doorbell would ring just after they had got the bottle down ready to take their dose. While they were paying the milkman or the window-cleaner, or just having a quick word over some domestic problem with a neighbour, their toddler would get hold of the pills, and stuff a few down. An official Report stated that there were between 15,700 and 16,700 children admitted to hospitals every year after eating or drinking adult medicines, and it was recognised that many more of such cases — probably at least double the hospital admission figures — were treated at clinics or by the family doctor.

I introduced my first Bill on this subject in April 1974, but it bit the dust when the Labour Government stonewalled, on the basis that a Report on the matter was awaited from a sub-committee of the Medicines Commission.

When the Report surfaced it proposed only that pills should not be made to look like sweets, ought not to be packed in bottles, and should be marketed in bubble packs or recloseable containers which would be difficult for a child to open. This was not enough, firstly because, although tablets and pills were certainly the main cause of medicine-poisoning in small children, liquid medicines poisoned too; and secondly, because the other remedy proposed by the Report was an expensive publicity campaign, which I did not think would work.

I was determined that only child-resistant closures would do the trick. The Report had turned these down on the asinine basis that (and I quote): 'the introduction of standard tests for child-resistant containers requiring participation by young children would involve showing the children how to open them.' The facts that one did not have to *show* the children anything — merely watch them to see if they could undo the cap — and that both America and Canada had carried out such tests perfectly successfully, seemed to be ignored by the Report.

So I introduced my second Safety Packaging for Medicines Bill, on 10 December 1974. I had made a slight alteration: the initial Bill had alarmed a number of organisations working for the elderly, the disabled and arthritic. It was, rightly, felt that some *adult* people might not be able to open the bottles — and indeed the measure *has* irritated many who struggle with opening aspirin and other bottles that contain medication harmful to children. I therefore now included a Clause to ensure that those who needed such medicine, yet had weak or deformed hands, could be exempted from having their remedies placed in child-resistant bottles. I made a special appeal to the Minister of Health, one Dr David Owen, and I stressed the dangers of delay. I was given leave to proceed. The Government itself then took over my Bill and it became law.

Some time later I was made aware, partly from a constituency case, that a grossly unfair situation existed with regard to nationality rights. If a British man married (say) a German woman and went to live in Hamburg, their children would automatically be British. But if a British woman married a German man and went to live in Germany, her children would have no such right to British citizenship.

I have never been of the strident feminist persuasion. Merit usually pushes a woman on and up, even if it is a bit more difficult for a woman to climb. I am uneasy about the advantages women have lost since sex equality, and more recently since positive discrimination became common practice. We can no longer even think of suggesting that a man treat a woman with special care and consideration, since we now must accept that the concept of 'the weaker sex' is an antiquated fancy; instead, it is decreed that a woman shall fight her own corner, and self-defence and assertiveness courses for women are available everywhere, to help them to do so. I rather think I preferred chivalry — it was more fun.

Despite my doubts about the pursuit of sex equality, I did think things — especially in law — should be *fair*: not at all the same thing as their being *equal*. It was not *fair* to prevent a woman from passing on her nationality to her child — even where both she and the father wished it done. Yet this was the position. It seemed totally wrong to me, and I determined to do something about it.

Examples of the gross unfairness of the rule were legion. One girl, married to a Norwegian, almost lost her baby when, at a very late stage in her pregnancy, she crossed the North Sea, which was so rough at the time that she was dreadfully sick. The only thing a girl *could* do if she wanted British nationality for her child was to come back to Britain for the birth, and a lot of these girls did that. It cost them money often they could not afford, and it robbed them of their husband's presence just when they needed it most.

Again I reached for the Ten-Minute Rule procedure. Again I was given leave to proceed, again the Government took up the cause, and the law was changed.

Technically, it is possible to introduce a Private Member's Bill during the Adjournment Debates for Christmas, Easter and the Summer Recess. But there is virtually no hope of it getting anywhere. I tried this out in the Easter Adjournment Debate in April 1977 when I sought, and got, leave to bring in a Bill to make regulations with regard to pre-release hostels.

There was such a hostel at Winson Green prison in Birmingham. Security there was practically nil. The theory was sound enough: these hostels would take prisoners who were shortly to leave the prison system, and allow them to acclimatise themselves gradually to living in the outside world again. They still operate. By no means all prisoners are permitted to take advantage of pre-release, only those who are judged to be suitable. They go out to work in the ordinary way and return to the hostel in the evenings.

All was far from well at Winson Green's pre-release hostel. After the men returned at the end of their working day they were allowed to go out again during the evening, the rule being that they must be back by 10:30 p.m., when, according to regulations, the hostel would be locked. However, at this time of night there was only one prison officer on duty, and the men would find a locked door no obstacle at all. They would simply open a window and be off to sample the various facets of Birmingham's night-life – including a little light burglary if the fit took them.

One such man got out after 10:30 p.m., stole a car, got drunk and broke into four houses. People were at home in two of the houses and he held them at knife-point and terrorised them. One couple had an 18-year-old daughter whom the man tried to rape, threatening her with a knife. There was a struggle in which both the prisoner and the girl were badly cut. Bleeding, he ran off to the sanctuary of the hostel, climbing undetected back through the window and into bed. The police investigated, checking the Criminal Records file. The evidence pointed unerringly to the prisoner in Winson Green, identified by both blood stains and by his appearance. But ... the man was undeniably in prison, ergo he couldn't have done it.

Later the same man fled to Bath, and again using a knife, broke into a house where he raped and stabbed to death a woman of 78. This time the police did get him. At his trial he asked for 34 other cases of burglary to be taken into consideration, *all* carried out while he was on pre-release. The system was operating as a licence to commit crime.

It was not as if this case was the only one highlighting the dangers of the pre-release system as it then stood. At the very time I was pleading for something to be done, two other men were awaiting trial at Warwick Crown Court accused of robbery with violence while on pre-release; then there was one awaiting trial in Stafford Crown Court, while two others had murdered a policeman in Reading in the same circumstances.

My Bill to regulate pre-release hostels got nowhere *as a bill*, the Parliamentary timing not being right. But because of the publicity for my efforts, and the newspaper reports which so strongly fortified my demands for changes, the regulations were altered, the prison authorities began to be a great deal more careful, and the numbers of troublesome incidents tumbled.

The next Bill which I initiated caused some hot controversy. For some nine years I had been Chairman of the Lords and Commons Family & Child Protection Group. This committee studied and sought evidence on any matter which it was thought might adversely affect children or further harm the institution of marriage, which all of us firmly believed was the vital cornerstone in any society, and certainly in ours. The Group worked quietly, mostly behind the scenes. In examining and pin-pointing potential dangers, it would lobby Ministers; and measures, such as, for instance, a change in tax rules which made it financially advantageous *not* to get married, were debated.

For some time the Group had been receiving extremely worrying information about the way that certain left-wing councils were actively promoting homosexuality and lesbianism in schools and even in pre-school nursery classes to some children as young as four and five years of age. Parents who dared to object were being physically abused and attacked. One pregnant woman lost the child she was carrying after a man who resented her objections kicked her in the stomach. It was reported in the London *Evening Standard* that gay and lesbian books were given to children in Lambeth Play Centres and Local Authority Children's Homes. *The Sun* drew attention to Lewisham Council's grant of £2,000 to an under-age gay organisation at the same time that it had cancelled a grant of £105 to the NSPCC. The Inner London Education Authority's resource list included a book called *The Milkman's on his way* which featured explicit sexual details of intercourse between a teenager and his homosexual adult lover, and several papers featured the front cover of a book showing a little girl of six sitting up in bed with her naked father on one side and his naked male lover on the other.

It was decided that our Group would introduce a Bill to end this perversion of children's minds, and that it should start in the Lords. My vice-chairman, the Earl of Halsbury, and Lord Campbell of Alloway undertook to draft and introduce the Bill. They were as good as their word, and the Bill was successfully launched in 'the other place'. But the General Election was looming, and time was very short. On the very last Friday possible — 8 May 1987 — I introduced the innocuous-sounding Local Government Act 1986 (Amendment) Bill. Until I got up to speak, Her Majesty's Opposition had no idea what the Bill was about: it was plain they had not even read it. Hardly any of them were there anyway; they (and a number of our side) were away to plan their hustings programme.

Labour's front-bench spokesman, Mr Alf Dubs from Battersea, realised in the nick of time that this was a Bill of which his Party was likely to disapprove. It had had a Committee Stage and a Report Stage in the Lords. It had passed its Second Reading in our House without any notice being taken — and if something wasn't done it could be on its last stage to becoming law that very afternoon! Mr Dubs acted. He stopped the Bill in its tracks by taking all Labour members present out of the Chamber, and the Bill fell for lack of a quorum.

However, before the House rose to go off to the hustings, I obtained from the Prime Minister herself (having put a direct question to Mrs Thatcher about the matter in Prime Minister's Question Time) the assurance of support in getting the measure through in the next Parliament.

The Election took place, the Conservatives won it, and Mr Dubs lost his seat. How best to proceed? Should I try for a Ten-Minute Rule? Not a good idea: the subject was too controversial. Suppose I won a top place in the Ballot? Unlikely — I never had, in 22 years of trying. Besides, the Bill might well be talked out. No, I must go for an Amendment in a Government Bill. I already had a promise of Prime Ministerial support — a cast-iron, copper-bottomed guarantee of success, if anything was.

But *which* Government Bill? There were two possibles — the Education Reform Bill and the Local Government Bill. I sought advice from the mysterious and wonderful Parliamentary experts on procedure, who know everything and miss nothing. They pondered the question for over a week, and then came up with the information that the Bill would correctly and appropriately fit in as an Amendment to the Local Government Bill. Thus the famous Clause 28 was born. And it *was* famous, too. I was absolutely amazed, not at the sound and fury of the opposition, but at the ludicrous claims they made about the Clause. It would mean a ban on staging plays by a huge range of playwrights from Shakespeare to Oscar Wilde. It would lead to the beating up of homosexuals. It would mean the burning of books wholesale. It was a witch-hunt, a lynch-mob, a Ku-Klux-Klan. When the Clause got a large majority in the Commons, an hysterical youth burst into tears in the Strangers' Gallery, yelling that his life was ruined. When the Lords passed it with a similarly large margin, lesbians let themselves down on ropes from the Gallery to the floor of the Chamber, screaming and biting and kicking the attendants as they were removed.

And all because we wanted to protect children! Again and again, I and others of the Clause's supporters said that what adult people chose to do with their lives was their affair. Nothing in the Clause would harm them in the least. All we wanted was that little children should not have homosexuality taught to them as a way of life.

CHAPTER TWELVE

Ted Heath and the Ulstermen

IT was in 1968 that extremism re-surfaced in Northern Ireland. The Province at that time had its own Parliament, whose powers covered internal affairs fairly comprehensively — Stormont handled housing, law and order, planning and health issues. Westminster retaining responsibility for matters of defence and external relations, tariffs and trade, postal services and coinage. This gave the Northern Irish electors three levels on which to vote — for the 12 Westminster MPs, for the MPs at Stormont, of which there were 52, and for their local councils.

Mind you, not everyone had a vote in local elections. This privilege was only for men and women of substance — you (or your spouse) had to own or be paying rent for a property 'valued at not less than £10'. This rather odd rule was left over from the original arrangements made back in 1920 at the time of partition, when Northern Ireland and the Republic of Ireland were set up in their present format. The same rule had applied all over the United Kingdom at that time, and had only changed on the mainland in 1949. Northern Ireland was itself due to change over to 'one man, one vote' in 1971, when the next local elections were due.

1968 was a pretty turbulent time, and other important reforms were afoot in Northern Ireland. An Ombudsman was to be appointed to adjudicate on citizens' grievances. A better system for the allocation of council houses had been announced, as well as a programme for more jobs, which was aimed at spreading employment opportunities equally over all the Province. Furthermore, the Stormont Parliament had embarked upon a positive policy to improve relations with the South. Prime Minister Captain Terence O'Neill (later Lord O'Neill of the Maine) had taken the initiative in this, and invited

120

his counterpart from Eire to meet him in Belfast to discuss practical co-operation between North and South.

It was almost certainly these admirable and statesmanlike actions which sparked trouble. Britain's enemies have always struck at her via Ireland — it was even happening back in the days of Henry VIII. Now, here was peace and friendship beginning to break out between Eire and Ulster on an unprecedented scale. If it got far, the opportunities for using the cloak of Irishness to create mischief for the UK would be severely curtailed. It had to stop!

A so-called 'Civil Rights Association' was launched in Northern Ireland. There was never the slightest doubt about its aims. In fact one of its leaders, Mr Michael Farrell, announced that 'we do not want reform of Northern Ireland — we want a revolution in Ireland'.

On 5 October 1968, the Civil Rights Association made an attempt to stage a march into an area of Londonderry that was traditionally hostile to Britain. The Stormont Minister for Home Affairs banned the march; but even so, the very existence of the Civil Rights movement, and the threats they made, created its own backlash — chiefly from the Rev. Ian Paisley and his extreme sectarian followers. The Civil Rights Association organised another march, this time across Northern Ireland, scheduled for 30 November. Paisley and his adherents sprang into action, and got organised. On the day, a large loyalist mob poured into Armagh ahead of the demonstrators. The Ulster police kept the two sides apart for a time, but the Paisleyites were still able to stop the marchers from getting through, and eventually fighting broke out.

Thus began one of the longest periods of sustained and organised terror in the long history of feuding over Ireland. During this time, thousands have been killed or wounded, including an appalling tally of innocent civilians. Other countries, indeed other continents, have become involved. The

IRA, INLA and other groups have now become part of an evil network of terrorist groups across the world who help each other out in such technical matters as weapons procurement and bomb-making.

The Americans, millions of whom have immigrants from Ireland among their ancestors, have extremely strong sentimental ties with 'the auld country'. Anyone who doubts the importance of this connection should try visiting an American city — any one will do — on St. Patrick's Day. In Illinois, for example, they expend vast sums each year dyeing the great Chicago River emerald green! But while sentiment is one thing, knowledge is quite another. Precious few of those Americans who celebrate, march, dance jigs or get drunk on St. Patrick's Day have the remotest understanding of the real situation on the island of Ireland. Americans have donated and collected millions of dollars for organisations involved in the cowardly and ruthless killing, maiming and torture of ordinary people in Ireland, and sometimes in mainland Britain too. The folk back in the United States have not had the faintest idea that their money was being used in such a way, and certainly would not have wished to fund acts of terrorism.

I well remember one young man in Boston who earnestly assured me that 'IRA' stood for 'Irish Relief Association'! The contents of the collection box he carried, bearing those letters, was going for food and clothing for impoverished and elderly people in Ireland: a worthy cause, surely? His confusion, though, was part of a more general misapprehension. It took a great many years for the mass of the American people to stop believing that the British had mounted an army of occupation on Irish soil, and finally to recognise that the soldiers were, in fact, there to keep warring factions apart, and thereby preserve lives — both Protestant and Catholic. Another message woefully slow in crossing the Atlantic was that Ulster votes overwhelmingly to remain part of the United Kingdom, whenever offered the opportunity to express a preference. A little research would have shown all this quite plainly, but for so long emotion tended to block out reason. Even today, I suspect, it would be a rare event to find an American who could name the Six Counties of Ulster, or tell you why and how partition came about.

By 1973 it was becoming abundantly clear that Ulster's own security forces needed far greater muscle than they possessed on their own. The success of the terrorist campaign necessitated the introduction of a fairly substantial force of British troops. It had already led to the establishment of direct rule from Westminster, and the disappearance of the Stormont Parliament.

That change had come about following a meeting between the Northern Ireland and United Kingdom Prime Ministers, Mr Brian Faulkner and Mr Edward Heath, in March 1971. At the meeting, Mr Heath proposed that the British Government should assume full responsibility for the maintenance of law and order in the Province. Operational responsibility already rested largely with the army, and Westminster was closely involved in handling this; yet Stormont retained control of policy — an awkward and unwieldy arrangement. There was another problem, too. While the Unionists had been pursuing a comprehensive programme of reforms (including the appointment of the Ombudsman, a new housing allocation scheme, an Incitement to Hatred Act, a Declaration of Equality of Employment Opportunity and universal suffrage in local elections), the main opposition parties at Stormont had refused to co-operate, and were conducting a campaign of civil disobedience which included non-payment of rent and rates.

Mr Faulkner did not agree to Mr Heath's proposal, and he and his Government resigned. In the circumstances there was little alternative to direct rule from Westminster, although it was far from an ideal solution.

A number of plans for alternative governing bodies in Ulster have been mooted and rejected since then. Local elections in Northern Ireland are conducted not on a straightforward majority system as in the rest of the UK, but on a form of proportional representation. This has resulted in the election of a worrying number of IRA supporters, many of whom have served long prison sentences for terrorist offences. One such was even elected to the Westminster Parliament, though he never took his seat. This was Gerry Adams, who, 10 years and many changes later, became prominent in the peace negotiations.

Like many Westminster MPs, I have great sympathy for the Ulster people, and I have visited the province several times. Some years ago I stood looking over the high wall round Corrie's Timber Yard, in Unionist territory. The view included a council house estate in republican Andersontown, and I watched while a van purporting to contain bread and cakes turned on to the estate, apparently delivering bakers' wares. Coming to a halt, it sounded its horn in what was clearly a signal. People ran from the houses and were given guns yanked from the back of the van. There were soldiers standing beside me, but they told me they had orders not to fire or challenge unless guns were actually being levelled at them. They could only watch the transfer helplessly. That same timber yard came under heavy attack from incendiary bombs on the following night. A fire engine racing to the blaze was captured by the IRA who sent a radio message to the Fire Headquarters in Belfast that unless personnel already there stopped fighting the fire, all the captured firemen would be shot. They stopped. I went back and tramped round the sodden blackened ruins of that timber yard early the next morning. I was shown fire hoses which had been hacked through with axes — apparently a quicker way of stopping the jets than turning off the water supply. The firemen's lives were saved, but the timber yard was destroyed, and once again the terrorists had won the day.

As well as sympathy, I have the highest admiration for the people of Ulster. I have seen small traders who had their premises bombed time and time again, carrying on their businesses behind boarded-up windows by the light of paraffin lamps. Both Catholics and Protestants managed somehow to live their lives, under constant threats of danger from sectarian extremists on both sides. Northern Ireland MPs in the Westminster Parliament had to conform to the most rigorous security rules, living in what became more fortresses than homes. One MP was shot dead in Ulster as he held his constituency surgery.

Hopefully, the latest discussions will in time lead to the longed-for peace. Negotiations call for the highest degree of diplomacy. Each side is stiff with suspicion, but the public longs for an end to the killing.

There have been many attempts to bring peace about. Successive British Governments have repeatedly tried to solve the Ulster problem, but although there have sometimes been lulls in the violence, it has always until now been resumed. Civilians shopping at Harrods, bandsmen of the Guards playing in a London Park, people having a quiet drink in a Birmingham pub, an MP driving from the House of Commons car park, the young wife and baby of a British soldier serving in Germany — all these and thousands more have been murdered by the IRA. The attempt to kill Prime Minister Margaret Thatcher and the whole Cabinet resulted in a terrible toll of death and injury at the Conservative Party Conference in 1984, in Brighton.

There was never the slightest point in any of these deaths. None past or to come could influence any British Government to give in to the demands of terrorists. Again and again it has been emphasised that Ulster will not be handed over to Eire unless and until the people of Northern Ireland vote for that option. Whatever the new agreement now being worked on may include when it is signed, it will not be enacted unless the people of Ulster support it.

But I am going ahead too fast. I want to return to the Winter of 1973/74, which had not been an easy time for Britain, either at Westminster or in the country. There was trouble from the miners, who banned overtime and safety work. There was a State of Emergency for a time, with curbs on the use of electricity. War in the Middle East led to petrol shortages, and petrol rationing coupons were prepared. A train drivers' ban on overtime meant severe difficulties for commuters; and by January most of British industry was on a three-day week. The Commons was recalled and pressure grew for a General Election to be called. The main issue was to be 'Who governs Britain?', and since the public were undoubtedly becoming alarmed at the power of Communist-led trade unions to cause havoc, the Conservative Government was, not unreasonably, hopeful of winning.

Until that General Election, in the Spring of 1974, the Ulster Unionists MPs had always been an intrinsic part of the Conservative and Unionist Party. At Westminster they had attended meetings of the 1922 Committee and all other Party committees. They had accepted (and obeyed) the Party Whip, as every other wing of the Party did. So when Dissolution occurred in February 1974, all of us went into the Election campaign as normal. The seven Ulster Unionist MPs at that time were Willy Orr, Jim Molyneaux, John Carson, Jim Kilfedder, Harold McCusker, William Ross and Harry West. All seven were, as far as they knew, in exactly the same position as always — candidates in Ulster for the Conservative and Unionist Party.

Most of the Parliamentary seats in Britain hold their count on the same day as the General Election takes place, although there are a number of country and Scottish seats which delay counting of the votes until the next day, because of the distances which the ballot boxes have to travel. Over in Ulster the counts always take place on the next day.

By the time the Election arrived, it was touch and go which side would win. Towards midnight on Election night itself, as result after result was announced, it was evident that the Conservatives were likely to lose. Experienced eyes watching the progression of results knew that a high proportion of the seats where counting was delayed would return Conservatives. In particular, the Ulster seats were pretty well bound to do so. Even so, on the following day the tally of Conservative wins failed to reach the required figures. By then, exhausted and dispirited, we were watching the gains and losses by party groupings, rather than by name of constituency.

At 5:30 p.m. on 1 March the count was still going on in Belfast. As it drew to a close, Jim Molyneaux was called to the telephone to speak to an official from his Party HQ. 'Something very funny is going on, Jim', he was told. 'We are not being counted in with the Conservatives; we are being put in with "Labour and others".'

This news was almost unbelievable. Jim Molyneaux checked it for himself over the next few media announcements and found it all too true. Puzzled and disturbed, he placed a telephone call to 10 Downing Street. He was told he could not be put through direct to the Prime Minister, but he spoke to a Private Secretary and asked that Mr Heath should be informed at once that seven Ulster Unionists had been elected. He did not know at that time that Mr Heath himself had issued an edict to the media, telling them not to count the Unionists as Conservatives, as they always had done hitherto.

Jim Molyneaux never had a reply to his telephone message. And having ditched the vital Ulster Unionists, the Election was lost. Ted Heath had no alternative but to resign, and Harold Wilson became Prime Minister. The extraordinary thing was that, had the Unionists been counted in, the Conservatives would have won, though narrowly.

This was how the 1974 Election results looked:

Labour 301
Conservatives 296
Liberals 14
United Ulster Unionists (formerly Conservatives) 11
Scottish Nationalists 7
Welsh Nationalists 2
Others 3

At no time during the 1974 campaign, or even during the count, did the Ulster Unionists have the slightest idea that they were about to be disowned by Edward Heath.

After a weekend of feverish activity, the House reassembled in the knowledge that Labour was to take over the reins. When Willy Orr and Jim Molyneaux received their normal notice to attend the 1922 Committee, they went along as usual. Ted Heath was to address the meeting.

Mr Heath informed Members that he had had talks with the Liberals, in an endeavour to find a formula on which they could work with us, so that the Government of the country should not pass into Labour hands. He told a sombre Committee that it had been found impossible to reach a solution. Never, though, at any stage in his speech, did he mention the seven brethren from Ulster — two of whom were actually sitting there in front of him. Yet he must have known that with their backing he could have held on to power.

No more notices bidding them to the 1922 Committee were ever sent. Willy Orr and Jim Molyneaux took up seats on the Front Bench below the gangway on the Opposition side of the House, where, of course we were all sitting now. There was never any explanation to the Conservative Party as to why Ted Heath instructed the media as he did.

On the following Saturday, Harry West sent a sharp telegram to Mr Heath pointing out that, allied to the seven Ulster Unionists elected were four other Northern Ireland politicians — Bill Craig, Robert Bradford, John Dunlop and Ian Paisley, members of either the Democratic Unionist Party or the Vanguard Unionist Party. He made it plain that all 11 Unionists were perfectly well prepared to work with the Conservatives. There appears to have been no response, although a rather curious report is made in a book by David Butler and Dennis Kavanagh entitled *The British General Election of February 1974*, which claims that Mr Heath sent a telegram to Harry West offering them the Conservative Whip at this time. This seems distinctly odd, since there would surely have been little point in offering the Whip to those already in receipt of it. Other reports, that the Ulster Unionists themselves resigned the Whip, are strenuously denied by all of them.

The real reason for the exclusion, at such a vital moment, of the Unionists from the Conservative Party remains a mystery. There was, of course, the universal opposition of the Ulster Unionists, to the 1973 Sunningdale Agreement.[1] But on every other issue they had supported the Conservative Government faithfully throughout the whole of its previous term. It is astonishing that neither the Conservative Leader, nor the Chief Whip, nor anyone in authority in the Conservative Party, ever said a single word to the Ulster Unionists about their sudden exclusion. Many back-bench Conservative MPs failed to understand the true reason why we had lost the Election, and it took quite a while for the penny to drop.

As realisation dawned, however, that it was Ted Heath himself who was responsible, resentment against him grew. There were other reasons too: he has always been a prickly and difficult colleague, giving the impression that he neither knew nor cared to know even the names of his back-benchers, let alone the back-benchers themselves. He had a lofty coldness which only a leader of brilliance could have afforded, and he was not that. He disliked women intensely, and did not bother to hide his feelings. Even in the constituencies, where 90 per cent of the work is done by women, he could barely be civil to them.

On one occasion he came to speak at a dinner in the Grand Hotel in Birmingham. It was a black tie affair supported by all the Birmingham Conservatives, though arranged by Edgbaston, which was to say by my own immensely capable Agent, Keith Andrews. A room had been booked in the hotel for Mr Heath to change. As everyone started to arrive downstairs, Keith went up to fetch the Prime Minister. In the lift he said: 'I have forgotten my cufflinks, Mr Andrews. Can you lend me yours?' Keith immediately removed his silver links and handed them over. They were never returned. I have no doubt it was mere

---

[1] The Sunningdale Agreement to establish a Council of Ireland was reached at a tripartite conference in England attended by representatives of the Governments of the United Kingdom, Northern Ireland and Eire.

absent-mindedness, but poor Keith did not tell me of his loss until years later, when it was too late to jog Mr Heath's memory.

I used to find it difficult, in carrying out speaking engagements in the constituencies at that time, to give the correct measure of verbal support to our Prime Minister — which is rightly expected from a loyal Member. The formula I found was ingenious, since it accorded acclaim without inaccuracy. 'Mr Heath', I would say, 'is a remarkable man. He has gone to the top in four separate fields: the army (he had been a Lieutenant Colonel), yachting (he raced, and had won prestigious prizes), music (his conducting abilities were well known) and politics.'

In fairness, there were other achievements, which deserve to be noted. He took Britain into Europe. He reduced taxes. He took action to control immigration. But he was not popular, and, at Westminster in the corridors, the tea room and the Smoking Room, the seeds of a leadership election were being sown.

Throughout that summer, the Labour Party struggled on without an overall majority, and it was clear that another General Election could not be long delayed. There was deep unease about Ted Heath remaining as Leader, but it is never possible to switch leaders in the run-up to an Election. In the event we went into an October Election with Ted still at the helm. He made, in the view of many Members, a cardinal error by fighting on a platform of coalition. As with the dumping of the Ulster Unionists eight months before, he had sought neither advice nor agreement from the Party for this line — it was simply not discussed.

Many of us were opposed to a coalition, and as it turned out, the Labour and Liberal Parties also disagreed: it was never on the cards. It was never necessary, either. Labour won the Election, though by only three seats. This, however, was not such a difficult situation for them as it sounded, since the

opposition parties were so divided, and it was to be May 1979
before another General Election came.

An election for the new Leader of the Conservative Party, on
the other hand, now appeared a pressing matter. After Ted
Heath's second defeat, and after his call for a coalition, the Party
had had enough. He was advised by close colleagues to resign
with dignity. He would not. Keith Joseph was the first to declare
his candidature. He ruined his chances, though, at the same
annual event at which Ted Heath had acquired my Agent's
cufflinks two years before. In his speech, he claimed that too
many children were born to mothers at the 'wrong end' of the
social scale. Sitting next to him, I could hardly believe my ears.
How could such a highly intelligent man make such a gaffe?
There was, of course, a storm of complaint, and he withdrew
his candidature a month later. Margaret Thatcher instantly
threw her hat in the ring.

Other names were discussed. Airey Neave, later Margaret
Thatcher's campaign manager (who was subsequently blown
up in his own car by an IRA bomb), had at first offered his
services to Willie Whitelaw, then to Edward du Cann. On 4
February 1975, the ballot took place. The figures were:

Margaret Thatcher 146
Willie Whitelaw 79
Geoffrey Howe 19
Jim Prior 19
John Peyton 11

A stunning victory for a woman destined for a place in history.

CHAPTER THIRTEEN

Dear . . .

THE first task each day for most MPs is to deal with the morning mail. On average we get some 30 or 40 letters a day, and all must be answered. Many will involve writing other letters as well as the actual reply: the case will need to be taken up with a government minister, a local government official or an ombudsman (there are now 11 of these, all dealing with different types of grievance); or it might require a letter to a Housing Association, a prison governor, a school head, a utility company, a hospital executive or the chairman of a quango.

If we don't deal with the incoming pile daily, it will grow to horrendous proportions and become totally unmanageable. As with the clients at our surgeries, the variety of subjects covered is endless — and even the subsections have their variations. Hundreds of letters come in from animal-lovers; they may be about factory-farming, the fur trade, the export of live animals, methods of slaughter, the use of animals for research, dog wardens, rottweilers or alsations which savage children, or tax on pet food. If it is true that the number of letters coming in on any given subject illustrates the true depth of the citizens' feelings, then there can be no doubt about the veracity of the old accusation that British people care more about animals than children — a press report of cruelty to a kitten will always spark off 20 times more letters than will an instance of cruelty to a child.

One week I kept a record of the letters I received and their subjects. There were 23 on housing, five on animal matters, three about overseas aid, and 30 from people who wanted help with a range of social security problems. These last came in a variety of guises: housing benefit hadn't come through, or they hadn't got what they needed in removal payments, or clothes, or new carpets, curtains or furniture; there was one sorry soul whose pension book had disappeared into the maw of the DHSS, somebody wasn't getting unemployment pay while abroad, another was panicking because the gas board had threatened to cut them off, and somebody else had lost their Giro cheque. Then there were 21 letters about law and order, four from parents who were dissatisfied with the school chosen for their child, and two from people whose neighbours were making their lives hell.

The rest of the letters split into immigration cases, and various unclassifiable odds and ends. For example, one constituent's sister had been arrested for drug-smuggling in the Mediterranean. Another was bitter about her divorce settlement; another said her son wanted to get out of the Army (two months and quite a bit of correspondence with the Ministry of Defence later, the young man wrote angrily that he certainly did *not* want out, and to take no notice of his mother). Then there was the problem of the man in Winson Green gaol who was totally innocent of all charges against him (after a year or two as a Member I reached the conclusion that Her Majesty's prisons are crammed with men who 'didn't do it'), whose mistress had hopped off to Australia with another man, taking his money and the furniture. In another case, a husband had died while on business in America and his widow wanted help towards the cost of getting his body back home for burial.

Among the immigration cases was one man who wanted a permanent visa for his sister-in-law; another wanted his stay extended to finish a training course. Then there were people waiting for hospital treatment which had been delayed; a woman who thought widow's pensions should be tax-free; an objection to a planning permission granted by the local council; and someone whose daylight was being obscured by a tree.

As always, my mailbag also included a number of replies from Ministers, to be sent on to those constituents on whose behalf I had written to the Minister in the first place. Fortunately, these at least are straightforward and easy to handle. Sometimes I keep a copy on file in case someone else writes on the same topic in the near future, as it will represent the most recent official Government thinking on the matter — and that is usually the best kind of reply to give in such cases.

Then there were the general complaints letters. These epistles take more time to answer than any of the others, as they ramble over a whole range of concerns, from, say, the irregularity of a bus service to the high cost of TV licences; they might include grouses about vandalised phone boxes or broken public toilets, and sometimes personal attacks on my colleagues are thrown in, for good measure. Each point has to be answered carefully and tactfully. Others had written not so much to complain, but to inquire — perhaps about when such and such a law was going to be brought in, or amended, or abolished — or to give their opinion on matters that were topical that particular week or of special concern to them.

In addition, there were a number of special campaign letters. I get some of these pretty well every week. I will say that those who mastermind a letter campaign to MPs should be aware that there are effective ways to do this, and completely ineffective ways. The biggest waste of time, in my judgement, is to have a number of postcards or format letters printed, and just get people to top-and-tail them. The senders will usually receive a printed card in return, saying merely that the Member has noted the communication. The general view at Westminster is that if people can't be bothered to write a letter themselves, they can't really be all that fussed about the matter. It is even doubtful they pay for the stamp, and many times the envelopes are all, quite evidently, addressed by the same hand.

Only slightly less pointless, from the point of view of influencing opinion, is the technique of giving supporters a letter, and asking them to copy it out. The results are one up on the printed format letters or cards, in that such missives are at least hand-written — but everything else is identical, and hard-pressed MPs can be forgiven for answering such letters in bulk with photocopies, if there are very large numbers coming in. The *real* letter, from someone wanting to express a grievance or needing practical help, is, however, treated by all MPs worth their salt as a priority matter, and getting 20 genuine, individual expressions of opinion on a subject, taking the same broad line, from 20 different constituents, really *does* indicate a strong feeling abroad in the community, and cannot be ignored. So if you would organise a campaign, do it with a light touch; supply facts, but make your eager protagonists do some work and give us their real opinions, put in their own way. If a tenth of them actually do it, it will have been worthwhile.

MPs, being highly individual characters, have different methods of dealing with their correspondence. I was once sitting at a desk in the Library at the House of Commons when my attention became drawn to the chap sitting at the next desk, opening his mail. He would scan briefly each letter as he opened it, and either throw it in the wastepaper basket or put it aside in a pile. But there seemed to be three or four going into the basket for each one put in the pile, and I watched this process with growing fascination. When he had finished, I couldn't help asking him his rule of selection. 'Oh, I never bother to answer until a person has written at least twice', said he. 'Often they just pick up a pen and sound off when they feel irritated. Gets it out of their system, you know, but they don't expect me to *answer*. If they are really bothered they'll write again. Saves me a lot of time.'

This particular master of energy-saving techniques did, I suppose, have a point. We professionals *can* sometimes take our replies more seriously than the sender took the original letter. Once I found myself seated next to a famous agony aunt at a Women's Lunch, and we began comparing notes. I was curious as to how many letters she received, wondering how she coped with them all. She said she'd have two or three hundred in a normal week, but that the yearly average came out at 700 a week, because there were certain weeks when the numbers soared to over a thousand. These were often the weeks in winter when there were cold or 'flu epidemics. 'That's when people who can normally cope get demoralised and write in', she told me. I replied that we politicians see the same thing exactly — people get in the mood for complaining when the weather is gloomy, or they've been forced to take to their beds. Not nearly so many letters come in when the sun shines, and everyone is planning and taking holidays, playing their favourite sports, or pottering around in the garden. What my colleague in the Library was saying chimes in with this: many people write when their mood takes a downswing, and in a day or two they are on top of things again, and forget all about the troubles that prompted them to write.

My own inclination, despite all this, is to play safe and reply to them all anyway. I'd hate to add to their troubles by seeming not to care — it could be the last straw for somebody. How would I know which ones are that close to the edge? I know for a fact that at times I am felt to be their last hope.

I admit to my own quirks, however. Any letter addressed to me which starts 'Dear Sir' goes straight into my wastepaper basket. If people can't even trouble to figure out my gender, then they do not, in my opinion, rate a reply. And one other thing: I simply *hate* being addressed as 'Ms'.

Some correspondents clearly think MPs are psychic. We are always getting letters signed with initials only, before the surname. How is one supposed to know whether the sender is a man or a woman? If this were just another manifestation of the dottier side of the equal opportunities industry, one wouldn't be surprised, but the letter-writers get quite irritated if you don't address them correctly according to their sex.

Someone called L. M. Scubifgy once wrote to me; at least I *think* that was his name. On the other hand, it could equally well have been I. H. Lewsgig or P. M. Tsulfoj, or ... The possibilities were almost endless.

Paper puzzles (apart from the odd crossword) are not much in my line but every so often a letter turns up with a totally illegible signature, and I enter gamely into the spirit of the thing. I give the letter a going-over that would do credit to Scotland Yard, peering at the general calligraphy for clues, and occasionally even prising open the mystery by a combination of guessing and luck. The 'Scubifgy' letter, however, was typed, and gave no indication as to whether my correspondent was a mid-European émigré, an African student, a Polish refugee or, for that matter, a Birmingham-born man named Smith.

So how *does* one reply to such letters? Oscar Wilde, or Bernard Shaw, or somebody, once wrote a letter to a friend which, as I recall, went something like this: 'Your letters have a unique quality, in that I can never read a word you write. Letters from others I read and throw away. Yours I keep for years, poring over them, wondering, cogitating, guessing, construing what you could possibly have meant to say.' I could hardly treat my missive from Scubifgy/Lewsgig/Tsulfoj in that manner, though. He or she clearly wanted an answer, and soon.

Whenever bafflement stares me in the face today over cases like this, I cut out the signature and stick it on the envelope with Sellotape, above the typewritten address. There have been cases where the writer has taken the hint.

Television and radio producers of programmes outside the House labour under the delusion that all MPs are burning with desire to feature in their programmes. They are wrong. Only recently-elected or obsessively self-publicist Members have any such wish. Those of us who have been in the House of Commons a few years, and have appeared rather a lot on television, will avoid the camera (and the microphone) like the plague.

There are a number of very good reasons for this. Interviewers (particularly young ones) have apparently been trained to be as rude and hectoring as possible. They strive to portray their victims as dim-witted, hard-hearted incompetents, and they are adept at framing variations on the 'Have you stopped beating your wife' question, to which there is no short answer.

One also learns by experience that television producers care not a rap for the interviewee's time, convenience or comfort. They expect you to stand in pouring rain in a force 10 gale on College Green being lambasted with questions. They get you into the television studios anything up to one and a quarter hours before the programme goes out. They take it for granted you will travel almost any distance, produce an audience (dark threats of filling the seats with political opponents are made if you refuse) and cancel your engagements for the day at a moment's notice.

Local radio programmes ring you up at any hour of the day or night for an interview 'down the line'. This means that they connect the telephone with their studio and your subsequent conversation goes out directly to the listening thousands. Less than thousands, I'll warrant, at the strange hours they sometimes like to transmit my pearls of wisdom.

I am far from ecstatic about having my sleep disturbed by calls at such times, especially as I am then expected to gather my wits and give an instant comment on some news item read out to me by the interviewer. He may not be giving me all the details, and he will certainly not let me know what other opinions have been expressed, nor by whom. Many a Parliamentary foot has been self-placed in many an MP's mouth on such occasions. And there isn't even any pecuniary advantage, for there is, of course, never any fee paid for these intrusions at distinctly unsocial hours.

However, all these drawbacks to air-wave exposure pale into insignificance beside the heavy burden of extra work they impose, in answering the mass of letters which pour in after each broadcast. Only the downright rude and abusive letters from non-constituents (a very small minority) can be consigned unanswered to the wastepaper-basket. Supportive letters, those which offer further points in the argument, and those which ask specific questions, must have a reply. No wonder seasoned secretaries groan whenever their boss takes on a television or radio interview.

A number of letters come to every MP from people who are, as John Major once said, 'two sandwiches short of a picnic'. Here is a postcard. The anonymous writer sends me one like it about every two months. What am I supposed to make of it?

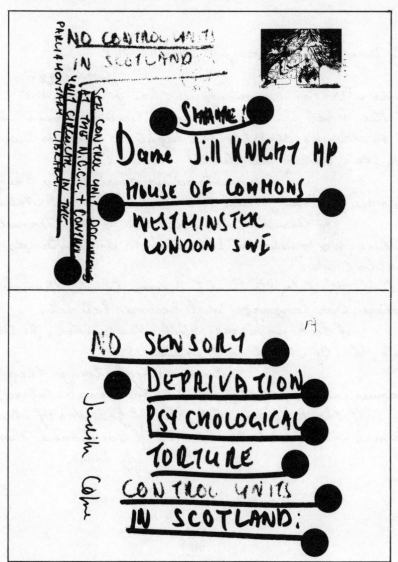

Here is a letter from a gentleman whose leave-taking is affectionate but whose purpose is somewhat obscure. Neither he, nor the postcard-sender above, is a constituent.

My Dear Rt. Hon. Dame Jill Knight, M.P.

Good Day.

Madam Do Parliament Agree That It Does Not Matter What Our Government Circumstances Are It Is Always Sensible And Right To Ask. Is Our U.K. Arts, Etc. Of An Eternal Nature?

Understanding That Every Thing Becomes Extinct, That Is Not Of An Eternal Nature

If Our U.K. Arts, Etc. Was Of An Eternal Nature, We Would Be Educated To Understand. — Wouldn't We?

If Our U.K. Arts, Etc. Don't Become Of An Eternal Nature, Our Language Will Become Extinct.

A Sick Universe, Will Never Ask. Is Our Arts, Etc. Of An Eternal Nature?

Even Though Every Thing Becomes Extinct, That Is Not Of An Eternal Nature.

If The Religious Arts, Etc. Of God Was Of An Eternal Nature. We Would Not Of Questioned Him.

All Of My Love,

Here is part of a letter from a would-be immigrant who put up such a good case to be allowed to remain in Britain that I did all I could to bring this about. However, I lost sympathy rather quickly when he refused to take the oath of allegiance. He sets out his reasons:

I am sorry to point out that the oath or affirmation of allegiance I am called upon to undertake seems quite antiquated to me.   Before I give some of my reasons for my inability to agree to give such an oath or affirmation, I would request you to allow me more time than three months already allowed so that this question of oath or affirmation can be fairly and reasonably settled.

My reasons for objecting to give such an oath or affirmation are not that I may or may not be against Monarchy - I have nothing against the present Monarch.   In fact I have a great admiration for the next heir, Prince Charles. But what about the heirs - born & unborn---after him.   They may be unworthy and the people of this country may decide to overthrow them. The civil war that may ensue may force me to be on the wrong side. This may look highly speculative but I believe one reason for insisting on such an oath or affirmation may be the possibility of such a situation. Besides,insisting on such an oath or affirmation only from certain sections of society is discriminatory.

In view of the above I hope you would not only extend the time limit but also excuse me from undertaking such an oath or affirmation.

Yours faithfully

Dated 4.1.1988

Then there was the milder, latter-day Guy Fawkes, who while not actually seeking to blow up Parliament, did send all Members a writ, reproduced here. None of us took any action and, as far as I know, none of us heard any more about it.

COURT FEES ONLY

Writ indorsed
with Statement
of Claim
[Liquidated
Demand]
(O.6, r. 1)

IN THE HIGH COURT OF JUSTICE   1988.—C.—No. 2149

Queen's Bench Division

[Sheffield   **District Registry]**

13 JUN 1988

Between   The CHRIST
                                                          Plaintiff

                                                   AND

                                 Parliament
                         (for members see attached list.)   Defendant

(1) Insert name.   **To the Defendant (¹)**
                                 Parliament,
(2) Insert address. of (²)
                                 Houses of Parliament,
                                 Westminster,
                                 London.

This Writ of Summons has been issued against you by the above-named Plaintiff in respect of the claim set out on the back.

Within 14 days after the service of this Writ on you, counting the day of service, you must either satisfy the claim or return to the Court Office mentioned below the accompanying **Acknowledgment of Service** stating therein whether you intend to contest these proceedings.

If you fail to satisfy the claim or to return the Acknowledgment within the time stated, or if you return the Acknowledgment without stating therein an intention to contest the proceedings, the Plaintiff   may proceed with the action and judgment may be entered against you forthwith without further notice.

(3)   Issued from the (³) [Central Office] [Sheffield   District Registry]
and   of the High Court this   13TH   day of   JUNE   1988.
nece

NOTE:—This Writ may not be served later than 12 calendar months beginning with that date unless renewed by order of the Court.

IMPORTANT

Directions for Acknowledgment of Service are given with the accompanying form

Statement of Claim

The Plaintiffs claim is for :-

1.   My rightful sovereignty over the United Kingdom of Great Britain
and Northern Ireland to be recognised by the Defendant.

2.   My rightful ownership of the United Kingdom of Great Britain
and Northern Ireland and everything thereupon and appertaining thereto
to be recognised by the Defendant.

3.   £100,000,000 Damages

(Signed)   *Christ - A.J.Hill*

within the time for returning the Acknowledgment of Service, the Defendant
pays   the amount claimed and £   146.75 for costs and, if the Plaintiff
obtains   an order for substituted service, the additional sum of £ 34.00 ,
further proceedings will be stayed. The money must be paid to the Plaintiff ..
Solicitors   or Agents

(1) If this Writ was
issued out of a
District Registry,
this indorsement
as to place where
the cause of action
arose should be
completed.

(2) Delete as
necessary.

(3) Insert name of
place.

(4) For
phraseology of this
indorsement where
the Plaintiff sues in
person, see
Supreme Court
Practice,
para 1.

(¹) [(²) [The cause] [One of the causes] of action in respect of which the Plaintiff
claims   relief in this action arose wholly or in part at (³)   Sheffield
in the district of the District Registry named overleaf.]

This Writ was issued by   The CHRIST - Mr. Anthony J. Hill

Plaintiff whose address   (²) [is] [are]
"The Way Home,"
P.O. Box 205,
Sheffield   S.1. 3.A.L.

oyez The Solicitors' Law Stationery Society plc, Oyez House, 27 Crimscott Street, London SE1 5TS

High Court A2A

1.86 F5793
5044027
* * * *

Titles flummox letter-writers. A Dame Commander of the British Empire is the female equivalent of a Knight, though still somewhat rarer. But whereas no one would dream of starting a letter to a Knight:

> Sir John Smith, MP
> House of Commons, London.
>
> Dear Mr Smith,
>
> . . .

almost all correspondents will write to a Dame:

> Dame Jill Knight, MP
> House of Commons, London.
>
> Dear Mrs Knight
>
> . . .

I have two other Christian names as well as Jill, and my initials are J C J Knight. How's this for an example of dim addressing?

Here is another example of stupidity or thoughtlessness:

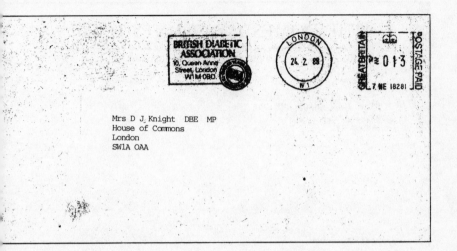

And even the Prime Minister's office can make mistakes:

And what price this one? Dame Obe, indeed!

THE DOMESDAY COUNTY FOLIOS

━━━━━━━━━━ BY GRACIOUS PERMISSION ━━━━━━━━━━
THIS OFFICIAL FACSIMILE IS DEDICATED TO HER MAJESTY THE QUEEN

```
Dame Jill Knight MP Obe
House of Commons
LONDON SW1
```

```
Dear Dame Obe,
```

And this correspondent cannot even recognise that a Dame is female!

```
Dame Jill Knight MP
House of Commons
London SW1
```

```
19 August 1988
```

```
Dear Mr Knight
```

    NEI direct exports from the UK last year, amounted to £207M out of a total UK turnover of £574M. A high proportion of this output was supplied against buyer credit financial packages arranged through ECGD.

CHAPTER FOURTEEN

Night of Decision

PARLIAMENTARY sittings start at varying times through the week — 2:30 p.m. is the norm, but Wednesday has a 10:00 a.m. start, while on Friday those of us not in our constituencies begin the session at 9:30 a.m. and finish at 3:00 p.m. This allows time in some cases for a Member still to reach his constituency office in time for an evening Surgery — but Fridays are, anyway, given over to subjects of a specialised nature, where only those particularly concerned or involved would be expected to stay to take part in debate.

All the daily Parliamentary sittings begin with prayers; attendance is usually pretty sparse, except for such occasions as Budget Day, when the House is full to overflowing — not, it must be frankly admitted, due mainly to the devoutness of Honourable Members. Maybe they *should* be particularly concerned to pray to the Almighty for special wisdom and judgement to help them to conduct such important business in a proper manner — but the truth of it is more prosaic. The only way we Members can reserve a seat on the green benches, since the Chamber is too small to seat everyone, is to come in early in the morning and place a prayer card, bearing our name, in the slot on the back of the seat; and even then, we have actually to be in that seat for prayers, else we lose the right to the place, card or no card.

The prayers we use are extremely old. We start with a translation of Psalm 67 which goes back to 1539, carry on with the 1637 Lord's Prayer (the old, familiar translation), and continue with a prayer for the Sovereign, derived from a prayer of 1525. The next one, the prayer for Parliament, has an extraordinary history.

Over 50 years ago, a Lord Hemingford wrote of a Select

147

Committee being set up to consider and settle the form of prayers to be used at the start of each day's sitting. Apart from Psalm 67, the Lord's Prayer and a prayer for the Royal Family, the Committee desired to include a prayer especially appropriate for use by Parliament, asking God's blessing upon their work for the Nation. The Committee asked their Chairman to compose such a prayer — a task he apparently found far from easy. He gave a great deal of thought to the matter, yet found himself unable to settle on anything he felt to be suitable and adequate. Then one night, he dreamt that an angel woke him and told him to get up and write down what he, the angel, would dictate. In his dream he did as he was told. The following day, when the Chairman met his Committee, he told them of his dream. The prayer, he said, was exactly what they wanted — the only trouble was that he could not recall a word of it! The Committee, much struck by the story, were adamant that he should return home at once and try his hardest to remember the forgotten words.

Back home he went, and straight up to his bedroom to think, and to pray for help in remembering his dream. A slip of paper caught his eye, lying rather untidily on the floor. He picked it up, and read, in his own handwriting, the prayer he now recognised as the one the angel had given him. Feeling a little foolish but relieved and greatly awed, he submitted the prayer at once to the Committee, which approved and adopted it without alteration. I do not know how this was recorded in the minutes, but the story stands, and the prayer is still said. The present Speaker's Chaplain, Canon Donald Gray, admits to some doubt about the truth of the story, but leads us in the prayer just the same. For my part, I see no reason to question the Select Committee's judgement of the matter at the time — that the prayer is an apt and beautiful gift from Heaven.

The final prayer is the one which used to mystify me — and, I daresay, quite a few other Members who happen to lack the benefit of a classical education. 'Prevent us, O Lord, in all our doings', it begins. I saw no reason whatever why I should pray for my doings to be prevented, and I didn't do so. Eventually I was put right on the matter; of course — it doesn't mean that at all. That awkward 'prevent' means (I quote from the *Oxford English Dictionary*) 'to go before with spiritual guidance'. The original writer was not, I suppose, to know that the word would later come to mean something so different as to be almost opposite, thereby making his short prayer utterly baffling. It is the best reason I have ever heard for revising the Book of Common Prayer.

At the doorkeeper's cry of 'Prayers are over!', the doors of Chamber and Gallery are flung wide, and press and public file into their seats, in a more or less orderly fashion, just in time to hear the Speaker announcing the business of the day. Question Time then ensues.

Tabling a Parliamentary Question is a fairly simple matter: one merely submits the question in writing to the Clerks in the Table Office. It must be done two weeks before the relevant Secretary of State is due to answer questions from the Despatch Box, thereby giving him notice of the question. A far more meaty and authoritative answer is thus possible than if the matter were unconsidered. Each Minister has his nominated day, every three weeks or so, when he must be in the Chamber and answer the questions tabled for him.

I was once told by a wise and senior Member never to put down a Parliamentary Question unless I knew the answer. It is not to extend one MP's knowledge that a P.Q. is tabled, but to probe, to embarrass, and perhaps also to get a column inch or two in one's local paper. The Minister will have the answer off pat, having prepared it. What he or she *doesn't* know is what *Supplementary Question* the Member is going to ask. It is the supplementary, not the main question, that holds the danger: the sting is in the tail. A Minister will look incompetent if he or she is caught out and is unable to reply sensibly to a supplementary. For that reason, every Ministerial department has a roomful or two of civil servants dedicated to working out

just what Supplementary Question(s) the Minister is likely to be
asked, given such details as the constituency, the record or the
inclination of the inquiring Member.

In spite of these little games, the rules governing Question
Time in our House of Commons ensure a more interesting and
informative period than Question Time in other legislative
chambers I have visited. And it is more orderly, too, notwith-
standing the shouting and occasionally loutish behaviour
deplored by many who watch the proceedings of the House on
television. I once sat in the visitors' gallery of the Canadian
Parliament. There were no pre-tabled questions, and no set
question-day for a particular Minister. All Ministers, Cabinet
and otherwise, were present, and all had to be prepared to
answer any old question flung at them from any direction. With
no foreknowledge, and therefore no preparation, most of the
answers had a sort of 'hit or miss' quality, and surely could not
carry much weight.

One Minister in our own House, though, is an exception to our
normal brisk commonsense arrangement. He or she has no clue
whatever as to what questions will come up and require an
answer. This Minister is, of course, the Prime Minister, who must
answer questions twice a week, on any topic at all, and all
entirely off the cuff. Only a bland request to list his engagements for the day is seen on the Order Paper. All the 'real'
questions are in effect Supplementaries to this one. If the token
P.Q. has been put down by a Member on the Government side,
there will possibly have been some liaison with No. 10, but
Opposition Members, and any Member called by the Speaker
during the course of the questioning, can bowl a very fast ball
indeed. The PM cannot turn to his officials for prompting; he
must know by heart such statistics as the latest unemployment
figures, how much money is going to overseas aid, to education,
to the National Health Service, to defence or to the arts. He
must be able to quote current pension amounts, road building

plans, inflation figures, mortgage repayments or afforestation proposals. He has to be acquainted with the views of a huge range of people — Heads of State around the world, Captains of Industry, Union Leaders, Chairmen of Trusts and other public bodies, Council Leaders and so on — as well as MPs.

All this is difficult enough, but when you add the 'home front' aspect of the PM's job — the need to know each Member's character, pet topics and foibles, and the name, location and chief features of his or her constituency — the true scale of the expertise and knowledge required is impressive. Yet I would be surprised if any member of the public, watching from the gallery or on TV, appreciates the full extent of the professionalism and skill on show at Prime Minister's Question Time.

In all the years I have been in Parliament, the most exciting single day was 28 March 1979. We had a Labour Government, the Prime Minister then being James Callaghan, the man who succeeded Harold Wilson after his surprise resignation from the premiership in April 1976. At the previous General Election in October 1974, Labour had held 319 seats, the Conservatives 276. Labour had been able to form a Government with a majority of a mere four seats over all other parties, helped in no small measure by the earlier episode in which Ted Heath lost the Conservatives the loyal support of the Ulster Unionists. As time rolled on, what with by-election losses and defections, this slim majority for Labour had been transformed into a *minority of 19* by March 1979, and Labour was only holding onto office by the doubtful virtue of a number of deals with various minority parties.

The Winter of 1978/79 had been a time of industrial unrest unmatched since the General Strike some 50 years before. Nine and a half million working days had been lost; there were strikes in factories, bakeries, local government offices, the coal mines and the railways. Ports and food depôts were picketed. Schools were closed and roads blocked with uncollected rubbish. Grieving relatives had to dig the graves for their dead.

Birmingham and the West Midlands were particularly hard hit. And what made it worse was that the region was totally unused to recession. When other areas had had their problems before, Birmingham had always sailed serenely on, because of the enormous diversity of her products. Not for nothing was this centre of civic pride called the 'city of a thousand trades' throughout the growth of industrial England and until the second half of the 20th century. When one trade foundered, there were always others to take up the slack. Indeed, the West Midlands had been a Mecca to which other workers, from the distressed areas of Lancashire, Scotland, the North-East and Wales, had come in the lean years to seek employment.

Now Birmingham herself was in deep trouble. The multiplicity of trades had ebbed away as the areas became more and more dependent on the motor trade — and that trade was in the tight grip of trade union militants. The great factories seemed to be permanently on strike — and for the most puerile of reasons. There were strikes when a foreman swore; strikes over the timing of tea-breaks; demarcation strikes if a worker from one section touched a car-body in another section; and strikes when a militant did not like the look of a new supervisor. In one incident, thousands of workers had to be laid off when a dispute arose over six inspectors being supplied with boiler-suits.

Ten years earlier, in 1969, Lord Stokes, the Chairman of British Leyland, had set down some bitter complaints in his Report to Shareholders. He wrote: 'Our suppliers and ourselves have been plagued during the year by industrial disputes, many of them unofficial and many of them over matters of trivial importance.' This was how it was in the very first year of British Leyland's existence — not an encouraging start! The same sort of thing had continued solidly through all of these 10 years, so that now not only was the car firm itself in bad trouble, but the blight had spread to hundreds of small companies supplying accessories.

Inevitably, sales of British cars slumped. This was partly because the strikes made delivery dates and prices uncertain but also because their quality had slumped, too. A car made in France, Germany, Sweden or Japan tended to be cheaper and more reliable. Somehow, management and workers in those countries were pulling together, while ours were pulling each other apart. In spite of his comments in the earlier Report to Shareholders, Lord Stokes and his management colleagues seemed to have been slow to recognise how badly the industrial relations difficulties were affecting their product and its popularity; they tried instead to 'talk up' the traditionally high quality of British-made vehicles, a story which nobody but themselves believed any more.

Those were bad days for the average factory worker, who had no relish for going on strike. There were a number of 'We want to work!' demonstrations, but all too often decisions to strike would be taken at huge factory-gate meetings, by a show of hands. There was considerable intimidation and physical bullying. When the cry went up from the rostrum for a show of hands in favour of strike action, there was often great reluctance — but the workers knew that if the hand did not go up, the boot would go in. And in that disreputable way, thousands of strikes were launched.

There was one notorious trade union leader in particular — Derek Robinson, known as 'Red Robbo' — who cost British Leyland untold millions of pounds in loss of cars and loss of orders, with consequential loss of jobs in large numbers. Much or most of the cost of this running disaster had to be borne by the Exchequer. In 1978, Labour's own Industry Secretary, Mr Eric Varley, reported to the House that 'The cost to the tax-payer of saving British Leyland has now reached £3,212 for every worker in the company — a total of £800 million' — a very large sum of money indeed in 1978.

Hundreds of West Midlands firms went under at that time.

A particularly grim sight I remember was the scores of factories
around Birmingham which had had their roofs removed. Rates
had to be paid on factories with roofs on, never mind if they
were empty, silent and neither producing nor earning a penny.
So there they stood, with the daylight shining into the vacant
shells, silent memorials to militancy and mismanagement of the
economy.

Faced with all this, Margaret Thatcher, now Leader of Her
Majesty's Opposition, must have sensed an opportunity for a
winnable motion of No Confidence in the Government. But
when, exactly, was going to be the right moment? She spent a
long time considering, waiting and watching, before she called us
all to arms by putting that crucial motion on the Order Paper.

It was always going to be a gamble. Prime Minister James
Callaghan would, in any ordinary circumstances, be able to
count on horse-trading with the minority groups to enable him
to survive such a vote. Besides, the timing of a possible General
Election, which inevitably follows a No Confidence motion if
the Government loses it, had to be considered. It was unheard-
of to go to the hustings in the winter months — cold weather
and campaigning do not go together. So, Mrs Thatcher held
back her bid. In the event, it was not the extreme deprivations
of the 'Winter of Discontent' which gave direct impetus to her
attack. The Labour Party had espoused the policy of devolution
for Scotland, and the policy had been quite heavily defeated in
a referendum on the matter North of the Border. At moments
such as this, Oppositions reach for the sword. Margaret
recognised her chance, and threw down her challenge.

Throughout that March day in 1979, excitement mounted
until it was at fever pitch. No one in or out of the Palace of
Westminster knew which way the vote would go. People kept
rushing in with stories about this or that MP whose support for
the motion — or opposition to it — was in doubt: stories of heart
attacks, improbable-sounding domestic accidents, and Members

immobilised into indecision by a crisis of conscience, seemed to reach epidemic proportions.

One of the weirdest stories involved myself — in a secondary role, I hasten to add. Two days earlier, I had been in Strasbourg at a Council of Europe meeting. I was approached there under conditions of cloak-and-dagger secrecy by a Labour Member who charged me with an important message for the Conservative Chief Whip. If he could be guaranteed a peerage, he would promise to support the Conservatives at the vote! I had a very good idea how this would be received, but on my return, feeling I had little choice, I duly sought out our Chief Whip, Humphrey Atkins, in the Smoking Room. I am glad to report that the offer was heard and dismissed in one second flat.

But still the outcome of the vote could not be calculated. Everyone was doing sums on the backs of envelopes, recalling chance words which might feasibly have given a clue as to the voting intention of a minority-party member, or calculating the possible effect of some reported slight: might the victim still feel the sting, and choose to take his revenge now? The Lib-Lab Pact had collapsed, back in the previous Autumn, and the votes of 11 Liberals looked almost certain to be cast against the Government; most minor parties, and the independent members, on the other hand, had to be marked down as 'doubtfuls'. It had been 55 years since a Government had been forced to go to the country as a result of losing a 'no confidence' vote. Would fear of the unknown overrule frustration today, as so often before? Vacillating Members might well come down on the side of the devil they knew. There really was no knowing.

The general air of mounting tension and excitement was not tempered by the fact that the whole of the catering staff in the House of Commons were on strike. Not a bite to eat — nor even as much as a cup of tea — could be obtained from any of the dining-rooms or cafeterias. But if the catering staff were pursuing industrial inaction, the bar staff were not. Stomachs were empty but glasses were full, and re-filled fairly constantly. I must explain here that, due to the rules of etiquette of *Hansard* (if not the Sergeant-at-Arms), no Member of Parliament is *ever* drunk. He is 'tired and emotional'; he may even be 'over-wrought' — he is *never* drunk. In fact, it was a wonder that strong drink on empty stomachs did not adversely affect MPs that night, but I can honestly say that it did not — probably because every single one of us felt a keen sense of occasion: this was a night to remember. It was more: a pivotal moment in history, destined to have the deepest, most far-reaching influence on our lives and the future and fortunes of our land.

In the Chamber, the Public Galleries were so tightly packed that you could not have slid an Order Paper between them. The representatives of the world's press similarly crammed their Gallery, and every servant of the House who was off duty sought a position from which he or she might view the proceedings. The queues outside must have been long; I do not know, for I never left the Chamber. I was, like a large number of my colleagues, hoping to take part in the debate — and MPs cherishing such aspirations in *any* debate are pretty well bound to stay in their seats. At this most historic moment, unparalleled in 50 years, anyone wishing to speak would have had to be daft — or desperate — to get up and leave, even for five minutes.

Apart from David Steel as leader of the Liberal Party, Jim Molyneaux as leader of the Ulster Unionists, and spokesmen for Plaid Cymru and the Scottish Nationalists, there were 18 back-benchers called to speak in that debate. And I *was* one of them, eager, as you may imagine, to tell the House how ordinary people in my patch were hurting and frustrated, as a result of the industrial decline in Birmingham which Labour policies were so powerless to contain.

Winding up for our side was Willie Whitelaw, and he did so with a speech which — for him — was unusually blistering. Michael Foot, the then Leader of the Commons, wound up for the Government. Now we were ready for the 'off'.

Still no-one knew what the outcome of the Division would be. The tension was almost unbearable. As the division bells rang, the Chamber emptied. Our side scurried off into the 'Aye' Lobby, some looking strained and nervous, others already boisterous and invigorated with certainty that a General Election was about to be announced.

Our votes cast, we rushed back to our seats to hear the result. The minutes crawled by. Just before the tellers came to the Speaker's Chair, the Labour Chief Whip appeared from the Members' Lobby end with a huge grin on his face. He marched up and whispered something to the Prime Minister. It seemed that we had lost and Jim Callaghan had survived to fight another day. Margaret Thatcher turned white, and I think half the rest of us did too. But then, about a minute later, one of our senior Whips, Anthony Berry (later tragically murdered by the IRA in the Brighton bombing) came bouncing in with an even broader grin, holding up the forefinger of his right hand in an unmistakeable message.

Still we held our breaths until the Whips positioned themselves at the table. Tellers for the winning side are always on the right. Conservatives Spencer le Marchant and Michael Roberts took up that place — and our side erupted in cheers and triumphant shouts.

Mr Speaker had to call for order for the figures to be announced. Ayes 311, Noes 310 — a victory for the Motion by *one vote*. The place went mad — well, on the Conservative side it did. We cheered, we waved our Order Papers, we stamped our feet. The Government side slumped in their seats, stunned and grim. Pressmen took to their heels, to fight for the nearest phone, while the public in the Strangers' Gallery stretched their cramped limbs and made for the doorways.

The show was over, barring one final formality. Mr Callaghan rose to speak for the last time in his capacity as

Prime Minister, announcing that he would be calling on Her
Majesty the Queen in the morning, to inform her of the
Dissolution of Parliament.

There being nothing more to be done, MPs went off to eat, to
unwind, and to celebrate — or lament — a remarkable and
momentous victory.

There is one other memory of that night which bears
recording. In Parliament at the time was an Irishman whose
allegiance was listed as Independent Labour. He kept a pub in
his constituency in Ulster and his attendance at Westminster
was erratic, to say the least. It was rumoured that on occasions
when his vote was deemed indispensable, a couple of Labour
Whips would be dispatched to Belfast to fetch him. This time,
however, he had come of his own accord; but instead of making
for the 'No' lobby when the bells went, he sat four-square in his
place, arms folded defiantly over his chest. Later on, I passed
him in the Members' Lobby, as we were both leaving, and
could not resist asking him why he had bothered to come. 'Ah,
Jill', he said, with simple dignity, 'I came over to *abstain in
person.*' Only an Irishman could have said that!

From that night everything started to change. The General
Election which took place five weeks later — on 3 May 1979 —
gave the Conservatives a majority in the Commons of 44, and
Labour's share of the vote, at just under 37 per cent, was the
lowest since 1931. This was a fairly impressive mandate for
change, and the new Government under Margaret Thatcher set
to work with a will. Naturally, the achievement of having
produced our first ever woman Prime Minister buoyed us all
along and gave us a strong sense of the historical importance of
the times.

One of Mrs Thatcher's first priorities was to oust militancy
from the trade unions. Quite a significant number of the public
felt that the first steps taken along this road were too small and
faltering. Legislation was introduced to restrict flying pickets

and to provide funds so that secret ballots could be taken on strikes and elections to union office. But although it gave some protection to those dismissed unfairly in a closed shop, the Government did not *outlaw* the closed shop, and this was resented by many.

Those who expressed resentment did not understand the vital need for a 'step by step' approach: sweeping and drastic reform would have alienated thousands of rank-and-file trade union members. We could have had a General Strike on our hands if we had tried *that* — the very last thing we needed, after so many months of disruption and strife. No, we were Conservatives after all, and had to win the trust of the workers in industry, who were used to socialist rhetoric and thinking. In the event, though, it was so patently obvious to all the union moderates that it was in *their* interests to get rid of the bullying and the intimidation, that they were keen for us to give them the right to a secret vote, on whether they wished to go on strike, and on whether or not they wanted a closed shop at their place of work.

Still, some expressed less than full approval for the new Conservative Government's first efforts in trades union reform, and it remained a controversial topic. Support was pretty solid, on the other hand, for the determined and immediate steps taken to combat inflation, which had become a terrible scourge for every section of the community from old age pensioners to young marrieds, from industrial workers to professionals, from young people on welfare to peers of the realm.

Labour had, at the General Election, quite missed the point of how worried voters were about inflation — or else they were simply unable to help, while remaining true to their principles. Their manifesto contained at least 57 specific proposals to increase government spending — a sure-fire recipe for soaring inflation. There were promises to extend national-isation, too. No wonder the whole package was rejected by the voters. The new Government did what pundits had said for years was impossible: they turned back the ratchet.

And this taming of the old ogre, inflation, freed the Government
to carry out its radical programme, which was about totally
changing the direction of post-war Britain, reducing the role of
Government and restoring a free-market economy.

It was to be a long reign.

CHAPTER FIFTEEN
Some You Lose

ALL through my political career my husband Monty had encouraged and supported me, never complaining about my absences — although whenever I returned from an overseas delegation or a speaking tour, he would fill the house with flowers. Sometimes he was even able to come with me, though more often he quietly got on with working in his ophthalmic practice, where his patients adored him.

He and I always looked forward immensely to the long Summer Recess, and made great plans. As the June of 1985 slid into July, though, Monty was not looking well, and seemed to be tiring easily. We rang the doctor and described the symptoms. The doctor told us there was a lot of it about, and not to worry; Monty should take a couple of Panadol and ring again if the symptoms persisted. They did persist, and an appointment was fixed for tests at our local hospital. We went along together, full of hope that whatever trivial problem he had would be diagnosed and sorted out, so that we could get on with enjoying our lovely free time together. Our world fell in when they told us he had Leukaemia.

Monty entered hospital the following day. The doctors were very cheerful and positive, and assured us that these days lots of people could be cured. We believed them; perhaps neither of us could have got through the coming months if we had not. They explained the treatment, and the pattern established itself: he would go into hospital every two weeks for chemotherapy, after which he felt terrible; then he'd come home for a while to recover, to the point of feeling almost normal and well — when they'd have him back in again for treatment, and make him feel dreadful again.

The Recess went by in this manner. When the House

resumed in the Autumn I informed the Whips that I should need to be away from Westminster quite a lot. They were very understanding; but sometimes my vote was needed too badly — a three-line whip means we must attend, no excuses accepted. On some evenings I would have to leave Monty's bedside at half past eight, drive down the motorway, vote in the Lobby, and climb back into my car for the return drive to Northampton. They were agonising and exhausting days.

By Christmas he was doing, amazingly, very well. He had fought a valiant fight, and seemed to have won it. At the end of January 1986 we received the result of the test that was expected to confirm this, but instead all our hopes were shattered: the disease had returned, more rampant than ever. He was given enormous doses of drugs which made him feel infinitely worse. The following weeks were the blackest of my life.

He died on 26 March 1986.

The night he died there was a most violent gale, and a large tree blew down in our garden. Within a few hours, thoughtful and kind friends in the village had moved all the wood and all the debris. They knew without a word being said how the sight of that great fallen tree added to my despair.

Monty had been the most wonderful husband and my best friend. His encouragement and help were always there to rely on; his deliciously dry sense of humour meant that however difficult life was, it was always fun; and there could have been no kinder nor more considerate partner.

I simply did not know how on earth I was going to manage without him. In the event, there were three things which got me through the bleak and miserable time that followed: the kindness of my friends, the love of my family and the welcome hard work of my job.

My two sons were a great strength. For years after, Roger would rearrange his Thursday evenings so as to be at my home, with a light on, a drink poured and a hug ready to welcome me as I returned (sometimes very late indeed) from Westminster. He understood with no promptings that going into a dark and lonely house by oneself in the middle of the night is an unhappy business. Andrew, too, did all he could, as did both their wives, so that I was rarely lonely for long. The grandchildren — Laura and Annabel then aged four and three, and little James born only a few weeks before Monty died — gave me much solace and comfort.

The workload at the House, and in the constituency, continued to grow steadily. As Chairman of the Conservative Health and Social Security Committee, it was my lot to defend the Government's record on TV and radio, and indeed at various meetings dotted around the country. I had two campaigns going at that time, both health-related issues; one of them I won and the other I lost.

The first one was to plead for more use of computers to deal with the hospital waiting-list problem. I knew that some hospitals in my area had vacancies for treatments or operations for which other local hospitals had waiting lists. Was it beyond the wit of man to set the two together? More computers were indeed supplied, and they were used, of course, for many other purposes as well.

Waiting-list problems proved more difficult to solve than merely matching patients to vacancies. For a start, some patients are determined to have one particular surgeon, having been advised to that effect by their GP. Others are anxious to be admitted only to hospital A; hospitals B, C and D are not acceptable, either because relatives could not easily visit or because they consider them not as good as hospital A. As a matter of fact, they are often right: there is indeed wide variation in standards of care between different hospitals, and between different areas. This was one of the major reasons for the big review which the Government set in train some time later.

Unfortunately, this problem of hospital waiting lists is perennial, and it is difficult to envisage the time arriving when there will be no wait of any kind for patients. New technologies and techniques do help many back to health, but there can be no question that the more medicine can achieve, the more it will be asked to achieve. So many new operations have become possible in recent years, thanks to the ingenuity of doctors and scientists, that cures which would have been unthinkable even a few years ago are now commonplace, and because an operation or treatment becomes available, the public naturally demands that all who need it should have it — instantly! From liver transplants to hip operations, demand has escalated. Government opponents cite as an example of falling standards in the Health Service that there are waiting lists for hip operations — forgetting or omitting to mention that only a relatively short time ago hip operations were not available at all.

Transplant operations present another difficulty: a wait must often be faced because of a lack of the necessary organs. Even if any liver would do (which it won't), there is often no liver available at all. Perhaps a young person might die, say in a road accident, or by suicide, at the opportune time for our patient. It is still far from certain that the potential donor was of the right blood group to match the intended recipient, and in any case the organ can be used only if there is a donor card in the deceased's wallet or handbag, or if the next of kin is ready — at a desperately difficult time — to authorise the procedure. One way or another, there is a lot of luck involved, and no Health Service on earth could provide usable organs for transplant every time a need arises, with never any delay or disappointment.

Another complication about trying to make all these operations available instantly is that they are extremely expensive. Unless the public accept the idea that there should be virtually no limit whatsoever to the amount of public money being poured into the National Health Service, they must face the fact that there will be very difficult decisions to make, and some much-wanted operations and treatments will not be able to go ahead.

I did win my case for more computers, to improve usage of what resources there were available. The campaign I lost at that time was a plea that charges should be made for staying in an NHS hospital, where the patient could afford it. I did not mean charges for the medication or the treatment or the nursing care — just what is often referred to as 'hotel charges'. If even the poorest peasant in Communist China must pay something for bed and board, during his stay in hospital, I did not see why the suggestion of some fair system of charging was so repugnant in Britain. In Europe also, such charges are perfectly normal; but for some reason or other the Government stoutly refuses to implement them here. I could not help thinking then, as I do today, that there exists here a source of extra money for the NHS which a large section of the public would regard as completely fair — again, so long as those who could not afford to pay did not have to do so.

In 1985 the question of televising Parliament was brought to the fore again. It was already happening in the House of Lords, although there were disagreements as to whether this was a huge success or a sad failure. I opposed the televising of our House, not least because of the estimated cost to the public. I also felt that if Parliament were to be shown from the moment Prayers finish till the cry 'who goes home?' went up (an average of at least nine hours a day), there was a danger of boring the great British public to death. If it did *not* cover the entire time, then there was a danger of biased reporting as a producer selected this or that section to highlight.

I was wrong to worry. In the event, only Prime Minister's Question Time on Tuesdays and Thursdays is televised regularly, together with some Parliamentary Committee work; and it is done perfectly fairly. Televising Parliament is today widely accepted, and the programmes are avidly watched in faraway places. Sometimes viewers in America write to me about them. A woman from Omaha did her best to be helpful: apparently my blue-and-white dress looks superb, but 'the grey one always looks as if it needs ironing'. Well, I would never have known!

As a footnote, however, I must say that I wonder how many other members of the working public — lawyers, bus conductors, teachers, office workers or lorry drivers — would accept the suggestion that, for long periods while they are working, the beady eyes of millions of viewers must be on them. I rather suspect the trade unions would have a field day.

In the late 1980s an idea resurfaced which I had opposed with success some six or seven years earlier: that charges should be imposed for eye tests and dental checks. The previous time, the Thatcher Government had backed down on this emotive subject, but this time around they were quite determined to have their way, and nothing I could do would prevent them. To this day I feel that my arguments had right on their side, and regret that the Government were so stubborn.

When the issue arose for debate, I asked for, and got, meetings with the Secretary of State for Health, the Chief Whip, and even the Prime Minister herself, to try to explain exactly why such a move would be wrong. It was, for a start, the first time in the 40-year history of the National Health Service that charges were going to be imposed for a health check. It is much in the interest of both patient and Government that emphasis should be placed on preventive medicine, and there could hardly be a clearer example of preventive medicine than regular medical checks. Anyone suffering from a medical problem is far more likely to be cured if the trouble is diagnosed at an early stage, and the cure will be quicker and cheaper, too. It seemed to me madness to take any action which might deter people from having health checks. I have not, personally, the slightest objection to charges being imposed for medicines, glasses or dental work if the check reveals those things to be necessary — so long as the patient can afford it. But I feel strongly that the test itself should be free.

Every other health check in the NHS at that time was free — why just pick on the ones for teeth and eyes? Or was this just a prelude to a whole new policy for the Health Service? Were we to look forward to charges for cancer smears, blood tests, heart checks and so on? Surely such a policy would be bound to waste far more than it saved — not to mention the avoidable suffering and misery? Others felt as I did, and Amendments to delete the proposals were moved in Committee, but they were lost, and the Bill went to the Lords with the Government's intentions enshrined.

The Lords, however, are made of sterner stuff. They know a cogent argument when they see one. They threw the proposition out, and the Bill returned to the Commons without the charging clause, thereby presenting Mrs Thatcher's Government with a major problem. Should they bow to the Lords, knowing quite well that a significant number of their own back-benchers would carry on the fight against the charges; or would they slog it out, despite the climate of opinion, relying on the Government Whips' Office to exert the necessary pressures on those of us who intended to vote with the Opposition?

The Government decided on the latter course. By now, though, it was late July 1988 and the House was about to rise for the Summer Recess. The Vote would have to be held over until October or early November when the last remnants of legislation must always be completed before the Session officially ends. This timing gave me a possibly helpful respite. I was anxious to get a clear message to the Front Bench that there was strong opposition to the charges being imposed, even among their normally loyal supporters, and that it would be wiser after all to recognise this and bow gracefully to the considered view of the Lords. I therefore put down an Early Day Motion on the Order Paper. This is something any Member can do, by simply taking it into the Table Office, as one might a Parliamentary Question. Other Members add their signatures to it if they agree with it.

An Early Day Motion (EDM) is an expression of Members' views, nothing more. It can commiserate, congratulate, condemn or commend. It *can*, if signed by an astonishingly large number of Members, lead to a debate in the Chamber — but this is unusual; there is no compulsion on any Government to take a blind bit of notice. Moreover, an EDM can easily backfire. For instance, during the apartheid years, an EDM wishing a South-African-bound rebel cricket team good luck would instantly have an amending EDM put down beside it to the effect (couched in suitable Parliamentary language passed as acceptable by the Clerks in the Table Office) that it was hoped that any team traitorous enough to go to South Africa would rot in hell. If the answering EDM attracts more signatures than the original, the instigators of the original look pretty silly.

My Early Day Motion, set down on that July day in 1988, read:

> That this House affirms its commitment to preventive medicine
> and calls upon Her Majesty's Government to accept the Lords'
> Amendments numbers 30 and 34 to the Health and Medicines
> Bill which would ensure the continuance of free optical and
> dental examinations.

Some 60 Conservative Members signed. No amending EDM was tabled. The warning was clear, but the Whips were furious. I was taken on one side by the biggest and toughest of the lot and warned categorically that if I dared to continue leading this campaign, the Whips would see to it that I was stripped of my Vice-Chairmanship of the 1922 Committee and my Chairmanship of the Conservative Health Committee.

This man must have thought he was furthering the cause of the Whips' Office and thus the Government. He couldn't have been more wrong. In fact, if he had pondered for a week in pursuit of a form of words which would bind me to my fight with hoops of steel, he could not have done a better job. It is a poor sort of MP who can be persuaded by threats or promises to abandon a course in which he or she truly believes. The belief may be quite wrong — anyone is entitled to disagree — but if one believes it to be right, there is no choice but to follow it through.

One cannot entirely blame the Whips for getting tough; their job is to get the maximum support into the lobbies on their side, and whether they twist arms, pat heads, hold out vague possibilities of future advancement, or just plain threaten, their motives are, we all recognise, as pure as the driven snow.

It was probably inevitable that some people would judge my battle on this issue as merely self-seeking. I was married to an optician, they said, and only trying to protect his income. Considering that he had died some two and a half years before, the charge was a trifle unfair. But it was made just the same.

My involvement did indeed have something to do with my marriage, but not in the way they thought. Over the 39 years I had lived with Monty, I had learned a great deal about optics. I remember times when, testing a patient's eyes, he had found such a serious condition that he would drop everything, cancel the next couple of tests, fetch his car and take the patient straight to hospital. If the problem was a detached retina, it was vital that the person's eyes and head should be kept in one position, or blindness could follow. He corrected many a child's squint and, like any qualified ophthalmic optician, could spot the first signs of a number of serious diseases such as cancer, diabetes, heart disease and glaucoma, when he carried out an eye test. This early warning can often save lives, which is why there should never ever be other than help and encouragement to the public to have their eyes tested regularly.

Government spokesmen predicted airily that no one would be deterred by charges, and that, in any case, opticians would probably provide free eye tests within a short space of time. Both predictions proved false, the first because, although there were some exceptions (children under a certain age could still get tests free), many people whose income was only *just* above Social Security level certainly could not afford the £12 a test was to cost, and would simply have to go without. Pensioners were not exempt, even though the advance of old age very frequently means worsening sight.

As for the pious hope that opticians would provide tests free, they could hardly do this and remain in business. They have no way of telling that a person will need any treatment, until the test is performed. Occasionally, no glasses are needed, but the Optometrist still has to pay his rent, his light, his heat and his staff. It is unrealistic that he should give half an hour of his professional time for no return at all. And even if the patient does need glasses, he may choose to go elsewhere for them. Some four years previously, in fact, the Government had passed legislation dictating that opticians *must* hand over the prescription: the patient is entitled to go to any dispensing optician to get the glasses made up. It was made illegal to exert pressure of any kind to persuade the person whose eyes had just been tested to get his glasses or contact lenses from the optician who carried out the test. Some 25 per cent of all patients taking the test actually did take their prescriptions away with them and had their spectacles made up elsewhere — usually by a dispensing-only optician, who could offer cheaper glasses. Under the Government's proposals, therefore, the optician doing tests free would be working for no recompense whatever for 25 per cent of the time.

There was one more point in this complicated argument. Eye tests in NHS hospitals would still be free. Anyone wanting a test could avoid paying for it, merely by getting his doctor to write out a chit for the Ophthalmic Department of the local hospital. Mind you, it cost the Health Service at that time £28 for every eye test in a hospital outside London, and £30 or more in London. So, bearing in mind that until this legislation the Government had paid the ophthalmic opticians a mere £10 for each test, there seemed to be some odd fiscal reasoning going on.

My logic did not prevail. The Government stuck fast to their course, reinstated their clauses, and we now live with the results. Time alone will tell how much harm has ensued, but certainly the numbers of tests dropped after the law was changed. I lost my Vice-Chairmanship of the 1922 Committee, as I had been warned that I would. Eventually I was voted back into it again, and I never lost the Chair of the Health Committee, so the Whips' anger did not last long.

CHAPTER SIXTEEN
Chinese Mice and
a Washington Chicken

IN the Autumn of 1985 the Presidential Committee of the Western European Union, of which I was then a member, received an invitation from the People's Republic of China to visit their country. Red China and Soviet Russia, far from allowing Communism, which was supposed to be their common political ideology, to forge a bond between them, had grown to hate and fear one another. The People's Republic of China was anxious to get the message across to Western Europe that there were at that time some two and a half million Soviet troops permanently massed on the Mongolian border with China. The Chinese Government hoped that by taking a group of European MPs to see the situation for themselves, they would be able to make the point with sufficient force; and the WEU was the obvious channel through which to do this.

The Member for Warwick and Leamington, Sir Dudley Smith, his wife Catherine, and I were the only Brits, but the whole party of MPs from Italy, France, Germany, Holland and Spain numbered about 10. We were led by a Frenchman, Jean-Marie Caro, who was Chairman of the WEU Presidential Committee at that time.

We all met in Hong Kong on the prearranged date. I had arrived the day before, but my luggage had not. To date, I have had this traumatic experience five times on international flights, and the unavoidable scramble to shop for emergency replacements is never easy. I must say, however, that this task is much less of a headache in Hong Kong than in some other cities I could mention!

Our party travelled up to Canton by train the following

morning. (Why is it that so many places in the world change their names? It happens a lot in Africa but it goes on in the Far East, too. Canton, for instance, is no longer Canton, but Guangzhou — all very confusing.)

The following two weeks were filled with interest — and with deprivations. The people were kind and welcoming: the food was abysmal. We ate bear, dogs' tongues, snake and traditional 'one hundred year old' eggs. None of these are likely to catch on in the UK — certainly not if I can help it! Those eggs were eggs all right, but I cannot believe the bit about their age. I suspect they boil them a lot, dye them green, and lie. Marvels such as a visit to the fabulous Terracotta Warriors of Sian (dating from around the 11th century B.C.), a walk on the Great Wall of China, visits to the Forbidden City and the Monastery and Grottos at Bezikelike, were interspersed with long and extremely uncomfortable journeys in planes, trains and cars.

We arrived in a place called Cichuan late one night, and the drive from the airport was hair-raising in the extreme. There seemed to be millions and millions of bicycles, like a gigantic swarm of locusts. Cyclists wandered at will over the road and wobbled like mad. The trouble was, none of them carried lights, on either front or back. There were a lot of lorries, too, and even they didn't have any rear lights; goodness knows what the accident rate was — it must have been high, but they seemed neither to know nor care. Blind faith ruled.

We had one train journey which took 18 hours. The train was very hot and extremely slow. We slept in wagons-lit, in which the washing facilities were well below par. Brought up never to retire for the night until I had cleaned my teeth, I journeyed along the corridor to the filthy toilet which had the small merit of a miniscule hand-basin boasting one tap which dribbled intermittently. Coming back from this expedition, I bumped into Dudley, who, observing my toothbrush and paste, paled instantly. 'You haven't washed your teeth in *that* place, have you?' he said in horror. When I told him *some* risks were inevitable, he regaled me with the story of a colleague who had cleaned his teeth in an obscure African state and was dead within 12 hours! This did not improve my sleep, and I was faintly surprised to find myself still alive when awoken the following morning by hammering on the door. This, I may say, was at about 5:30 a.m.: the Chinese regard lying in bed after 6:00 as a capitalist indulgence. We were certainly not going to be permitted such a luxury!

It is strange the way the Chinese seem to have regressed in modern times, rather than progressed. They are the inheritors of one of the oldest civilisations known to man, responsible for the most sophisticated engineering projects (just look at the brilliant irrigation system in Chingdu, built two thousand years ago and still as effective as ever); they could paint and write expertly, carve exquisitely, and build magnificently, thousands of years ago. They seem now to have been overtaken by just about every other country in the civilised world in such matters as how to till the land, or provide proper lavatories, or keep cockroaches out of guests' bedrooms. In one museum we saw evidence that Chinese doctors were using anaesthetics in about 500 B.C. (There, and I thought anaesthesia was first invented by the Victorians!) And yet, as we travelled mile after mile through rural China, I saw the peasants ploughing with oxen in exactly the same way as they did in the wall frescoes and paintings we were shown, which were well over a thousand years old.

They are, however, self-sufficient in growing all the rice, millet, corn and other staple foods that they need — which is pretty impressive, bearing in mind their huge population. For them the simple, primitive methods are evidently perfectly effective. They are in no particular hurry to update them.

Our delegation travelled right across the Gobi desert to see those Russian soldiers on the Chinese border. It is a wild, stony place where constant winds blow away every scrap of soil and sand so that there is not a blade of grass, not a bush nor a tree. The sun seemed never to shine, as a dust cloud hung permanently in the air above us, cutting out heat and creating a subdued greyness everywhere.

The remote hotels and guest houses where we stayed had a uniformity about them, too, in many ways. A point which charmed me was the total absence of locks on the doors: visitors' belongings were quite safe, as no-one ever stole anything. A not-so-charming trait was the Chinese habit of doing what comes naturally, burping or breaking wind quite freely, whether alone or in company. They simply let fly whenever the fit takes them.

We stayed at an unforgettable hotel in the Gobi desert. The routine for arriving at hotels was by now something we could perform entirely on automatic pilot. Book into room, have a quick hand-wash, go down to the lounge for briefing. These lectures on local industries and activities were always done by the Chinese with immense efficiency, and, for our group of assorted Europeans, a corps of interpreters.

At this particular hotel in the Gobi, we followed the usual practice and hurried down to the lounge, where the big armchairs were, as always, adorned with antimacassars on the backs and matching strips of embroidered linen or cotton on the arms. I was just about to take my seat when Jean-Marie called me over to sit next to him. As I was the only woman on the delegation, he was always anxious to give me a chance to ask my own questions of our lecturers.

Sitting down, and glancing over to where I had been intending to sit, I saw a mouse strolling casually in front of the chairs. I utterly and absolutely *hate* mice. I always react to them in a womanly, if not downright cowardly, way. A strangled squeak erupted from my trembling lips. My legs suddenly tucked themselves underneath me on my chair. Clearly, concentration on the matter in hand was going to be more than a little difficult. Jean-Marie looked at me with disapproval. 'Qu'est-ce que c'est que ça, Jill?' he asked. 'There's a mouse over there!', I quavered. Pause. 'Walking about!', I stammered on inanely. I was not at my best.

He had little sympathy. 'Pull yourself together, Jill', he said sternly. I did try. But as the briefing progressed, the ghastly truth of the situation emerged. There were mice all around us! Some running along the backs of the chairs; some scampering across the floor or running up the curtains. And one or two on each of the various cabinets and chests which furnished the lounge. They had colonised the place — there must have been hundreds of them in that one room.

I abruptly lost interest in the petro-chemicals industry of the area. A German MP suddenly slapped his leg, on thigh and knee and calf. Out from the bottom of his trouser leg fell a stunned mouse. Everyone else — except the Chinese — lost interest in petro-chemicals. I suspected, and later found I was right, that whether in that beastly room or outside it — in the dining-room, in my bedroom or the hotel lobby — the mouse population thrived and no-one seemed to care a scrap. Except the foreign guests, that is.

There are oases in the Gobi Desert, and small sweet green grapes grow there in abundance. The locals make wine from these, and we had a most pleasant lunch under the vines at one winery there. This was much better. There were juicy melons to eat; the wine was cool and there wasn't a mouse in sight.

We spent a day with a tank regiment, watching manoeuvres and firing practice. The tanks seemed rather antiquated models but were effective enough. Four years later they were to be shown on TV sets all over the world, taking part in the ruthless crushing of freedom demands by students and others — the notorious Tiananmen Square incident. However, there was no hint, in those October days in 1985, of such troubles to come. Our group had meetings with Professor Huan Xiang, Director of the Centre for International Studies, and with Xu Xin, President of the Institute of Strategic Studies. We also met the Vice-Minister at the Foreign Ministry, Zhou Nan, as well as attending an important dinner given by President Han Nian Long.

They were, all of them, courteous and polite in every detail; but to me there was an unmistakeable air of menace — a ruthless disregard for individual rights, which is so typically Communist. The country was fascinating and often beautiful. The people were everywhere unfailingly hospitable and kind. Yet it was as if a great weight had been lifted from me, when the plane took off for England.

Tiananmen Square, 4 June 1989, changed the whole course of events in Far East Asia. In Hong Kong, confidence drained away in the certain knowledge that there were only eight years left before the Colony had to be handed back to Communist China. All the thriving free enterprise, prosperity and individual freedom which Hong Kong residents have taken for granted for so long suddenly had a 'sell by' label attached. A trickle of emigrants turned into a steady stream, and threatened to become a flood.

The British Government reacted with the Hong Kong Bill, offering 50,000 UK passports to selected residents, entitling them to come to Britain, bringing their families, if the worst happened and China made a Communist takeover. The feeling, supported by many in Hong Kong, was that very few would actually take up their right to move to the UK — but it would give them more bargaining power, more clout, in dealing with the Chinese. The Bill was widely recognised as an honest attempt to encourage key personnel to remain in Hong Kong, and stand up for the traditional free-market system which has done so well there for so long.

However, I could not feel any confidence that the measure would succeed, and was forced to tell the Whips that I could not support it. Others, too, felt that this was not really a workable or adequate solution. The man who led the fight against it was the prominent ex-Minister and former Party Chairman, Norman Tebbit. Despite this doughty opposition, the Hong Kong Bill passed — Government-backed Bills pretty well always do — and, as I write, it is too early to say whether Norman Tebbit and the rest of us rebels were right or wrong. Let us hope we were wrong.

My own stance on the issue was undoubtedly influenced by that Western European Union visit, not so much by the experiences, or the information, received, but more by the gut feelings which the trip engendered, and which remain with me.

China is unpredictable. Hong Kong knows that perfectly well. Even bearing in mind China's need for the free-market outlet Hong Kong provides, she may well cut off her free-market nose to save her Communist-dogma face. And there are millions more than 50,000 residents in Hong Kong. Will those who cannot be accommodated in Britain stay in Hong Kong? And if they do not, how can the Hong Kong we know be enabled to survive?

Three years later, just before leaving the WEU Delegation, I took part in another Presidential Committee visit — this time to Washington. It was short (five days) but intensive. At the State department in 'C' Street we discussed Budget Sharing, Soviet Relations, NATO Commitments and Arms Control. We had a series of regional briefings on the Persian Gulf, Central America, Afghanistan and Southern Africa. We also had talks at the Pentagon on what was then known as 'Star Wars'.

Just about everything we discussed on that visit has been superseded by the radical changes in the Soviet Union and Eastern Europe, started by President Gorbachev with his 'glasnost' and 'perestroika'; but then, defence matters never stand still. Armaments are altered by technical advance just as policy is dictated by changing circumstances.

There were two special memories from that trip to Washington. The first occurred during an all-day session at the State Department. I had gone out to lunch, taking the opportunity to meet friends and catch up on their news. Returning promptly for the afternoon's work, which was due to commence at 2:30 p.m., my way was blocked by a huge security guard. His brawny arm actually barred my way. Waving my security pass under his nose and assuring him that it was *bona fide* produced no useful effect.

He said *something*, but it was entirely incomprehensible to me. 'Sorry?', I replied, totally fogged. He repeated the same phrase. It was no clearer the second time. 'Aha!' I thought, 'they've brought in a new password since this morning and they haven't told me about it.' A frank appeal to the mercy of the guard seemed the best course of action. 'Terribly sorry', I said, 'if that is a new password, they haven't told it to me. But honestly, I've got to get into the conference room. Here is my pass. Here is my passport. Here is my driving licence. Here is my airline ticket.' Desperation loomed.

He looked at me sorrowfully. A hand like a black ham smote his chest with some force. 'Ma'am', he said, in a most delightful Southern accent, 'ma indigestion is killin' me.' The phrase which had so mystified me turned out to have been: 'Ma'am, do you have any Tums Rolls?'

'Tums Rolls', it appears, are a sort of American Bisodol, Setlers, or Milk of Magnesia. He could have asked me for any of those, but who had ever heard of Tums Rolls? Only Americans ...

As he let me through, I just had to query, curious to the last, what had made him ask *me* — there were lots of people coming through his security gate, so why had he stopped me and not one of them? He gave me a sad smile. 'Ma'am, you got a kind face', he said. It was somehow such an endearing and human-ising touch. Even the great Washington State Department can falter for want of a Tums Roll! Never in the world would a Chinese security guard halt an Official Visitor to ask for an indigestion tablet. Nor, I think, would a British one in Whitehall.

Security at the Pentagon was hardly a more serious matter, though it certainly had all the hallmarks. All 10 of us trooped in one morning to keep an appointment with the Chief of Staff. We were vetted at Security Desk No. 1 and pronounced harmless. At Security Desk No. 2 our credentials were checked again and we were allowed to pass. But Security Desk No. 3 was unmanned and we were told to wait. We waited five minutes, then 10. Just as we were beginning to fear that we would be late for our top-level appointment, the most extraordinary thing happened. Through the swing-doors came a six-foot chicken, wearing baseball socks and carrying a bunch of balloons. It had a prominent beak and tail feathers of an amazing hue. Straight past Security Desk No. 1 it strode. It ignored Security Desk No. 2 as the guard there gave it a bored glance. Unmanned Security Desk No. 3 might not even have existed for all the notice taken of it by this exotic fowl. Straight into the elevator it went and disappeared.

We gazed at this apparition open-mouthed. 'Wh ... wh ... what was that?' we queried of the bored guard. He shifted his chewing-gum from one side of his face to the other. 'Aw gee', he said, 'it'll just be some Four Star General has a birthday.' He returned to his reading matter.

We pondered the apparent fact that for anyone wanting to blow up the Pentagon or take out a Four Star General, the really essential kit was a chicken outfit, a dozen balloons, and a pair of baseball socks.

CHAPTER SEVENTEEN

'If You Can't Stand the Heat...'

THE charge is occasionally levelled at us that modern Parliaments do not have the colourful personalities which so ornamented and enhanced Parliamentary life in former times. Don't they?

There is Dennis Skinner, all belligerency and yellow socks; Andrew Faulds who looks and sounds more and more like an Old Testament Prophet as the years go on; Ian Paisley, the thundering man-mountain in a dog-collar; David Evans, Rhodes Boyson and the great Nicholas Soames. Personalities every one, and there are many more. Some entered Parliament having already made their names in a different field, but the House is another matter; success in one job is far from a guarantee that the high-flyer will also shine at Westminster.

John Davies, for example, was an enormously successful businessman who had been Director-General of the Confederation of British Industry in the 1960s. In June 1970 he was elected as Member of Parliament for Knutsford in Cheshire. With breathtaking speed he shot up the ministerial ladder, becoming Minister of Technology in July 1970. By October of that year he was a Cabinet Minister — Secretary of State for Trade and Industry and President of the Board of Trade, no less. But somehow he could not transplant his old flair. His discomfort at the Dispatch Box was plain to see. Board meetings in the City had been no problem: fielding hostile questions from Her Majesty's Opposition in Parliament was quite another matter.

On the Labour side, Frank Cousins had been a man of stature and importance as a trade union leader. As a Parliamentarian, and a Minister, he was, I am sorry to say, a disaster. Glenda Jackson left a glittering career as a famous star of films and television, to become a very plain and very ordinary back-bencher; Ken Livingstone also glittered brightly when leader of the Greater London Council, yet once ensconced on the back benches in Parliament, he has seemed to generate no more than the odd flicker of interest. That is a long way from being a 'failure', of course — it's just that being a 'personality' in the House is a curiously different thing from being one elsewhere. I am quite unable to define this difference: I merely note it.

The worst hazard to face a politician is, without doubt, bitterness. For some, who have entered Parliament setting their sights firmly on the red boxes and the black cars of high office, it is gall and wormwood when promotion does not come. Many a good man has allowed bitterness to eat into his soul like a canker and the process is obvious to the onlooker, and disastrous for the embittered.

The clearest example of this is that remarkable and erudite man, Enoch Powell. A man of brilliance. A star in the Parliamentary firmament. Listening to him make a speech was to hear a master at work. Never a note, and yet with every argument marshalled and delivered with perfection.

Sacked from the Front Bench by Ted Heath in April 1968 for his so-called 'Rivers of Blood' speech on immigration, he became more bitter every day as he brooded from the back benches. Enoch Powell was never self-opinionated, but he knew perfectly well that his IQ was far in excess of almost every Minister on the Front Bench at the time, and it galled him.

When bitterness takes root, it destroys judgement and political acumen. Had Enoch simply ceased to take the Conservative Whip and become, as others had done before him, an Independent Conservative, his whole political career could have revived. Instead of this, he abruptly left the Commons and went, of all places, to Northern Ireland — where he was returned as an Ulster Unionist for South Down in the 1974 General Election. He had no need to go to Ireland. His old constituents in Wolverhampton South-West would have elected him whatever he stood as. He could have remained as the Independent Conservative MP for that constituency for as long as he wished and he would certainly never have been defeated, as later happened to him in Northern Ireland.

But even worse than leaving the Party, he blighted his future chances beyond redemption by telling people, in his speeches at the 1974 General Election, to vote Labour. Since the whole of the row which led to his sacking had come about because of his strong feelings that immigration into Britain should stop, it seemed extremely odd that he should support and encourage a Labour victory. Labour had refused to condemn further immigration into Britain, and, without question, would undoubtedly permit very much more of it, if they were elected to govern. But by then Enoch had switched horses. Apparently he was no longer concerned so much about the immigration issue as the Common Market issue. He objected to Britain's entry, which the Conservatives supported and the Labour Party did not. And, when I asked him how he could have encouraged a Labour victory, bearing in mind their stance on immigration, that was the answer I got.

Enoch remained as an Ulster Unionist Member of Parliament until he was defeated in the General Election of 1987. Perhaps he would never have made a good Minister again. Perhaps the Conservative Party did not lose very greatly by his self-imposed banishment. But his was a classic example of how bitterness destroys judgement. Entirely by his own action, he debarred himself from high office. Had he remained loyal and, in due course, asked to receive the Conservative Whip again, he would probably have returned to office.

Lesser lights, similarly disappointed at not being made a Minister, or because they were sacked from office, have displayed the same bitterness. Among their ranks one finds the conspirators, the malcontents, and the grumblers. They plot against the Prime Minister, whoever he (or she) may be. They make impassioned anti-Government speeches which delight the Opposition. The tragic thing is that they harm themselves more than anyone else.

It is a very great honour to be a Member of Parliament at all. To carry on the tradition whose roots lie in ancient history; to be at the hub of British political life; to be in a position to influence policy, even to pass laws; to be able to take positive steps to help constituents in need — all these and other things which make up the job of an MP ought, surely, to be enough in themselves. It is sad when they are not.

All sorts of things influence whether or not one becomes a Minister. Not being in the magic circle; the wrong speech at the wrong time; voting against the Whips' directives; acquiring the reputation of being a non-team player — all these can affect ascent up the greasy pole of political advancement. In my case it was undoubtedly detrimental that during the period when I might have looked for promotion, Mr Edward Heath was Prime Minister. He thoroughly disliked women and only ever promoted one.

A piece of inaccurate and unjust publicity may have been harmful to me, too.

In 1974 a woman named Nesta Wyn Ellis wrote a book called 'Dear Elector', which, amazingly, she had subtitled 'The Truth about MPs'. I say 'amazingly' because what she wrote about *me* was certainly a lie. Unfortunately, I knew nothing of this when the book was published, and she had not had the courtesy to check with me about the allegations she made. I had neither heard of the book nor read it; and it was not until six years later that a friend and colleague of mine, Denshore Dover, asked me if I had seen this book, and later forwarded his copy to me saying he had no wish to have it on his bookshelves.

In her book she noted that *The Times* of 4 May 1971 contained an advertisement which ran:

> Urgently wanted: a British MP to go to East Pakistan for a survey of the situation as seen by the Army and report back to the British public. All expenses paid.

Nesta Wyn Ellis went on to say that three Members of
Parliament had replied to the advertisement, offering to go.
These were, so she said, James Tinn from the Labour benches,
Jim Kilfedder, an Ulster Unionist, and myself.

The truth was that, far from replying to the advertisment,
none of us had ever seen it — and none of us knew anything
about it. We had all indeed visited Pakistan, but at the personal
request of a colleague who had many years of family
connections with the country, and who was Chairman of the
All-Party Pakistan Group in the House. Following many years
of disputes and occasional violent clashes with India over the
status of Kashmir and other matters, the political situation in the
whole of Pakistan was highly unstable — and East Pakistan was
in a state of near-anarchy.

The country's President, Yahya Khan, had sent all foreign
reporters out of Pakistan, and no news was coming from that
country, although there were plenty of rumours and allegations
from Pakistan's enemies. We were therefore invited to go and
see for ourselves, and I agreed to write what I saw, for *The Daily
Telegraph*. This in itself should have alerted Nesta Wyn Ellis to
her inaccuracy — for surely if I *had* responded to *The Times*'s
advertisment, I would have written for them and not *The Daily
Telegraph*. Anyway, I did exactly as I had promised: I went, I
saw, and what I saw went into my report, without embellish-
ment or supposition. I was very careful about this, and all I
wrote was endorsed as factual by James Tinn and Jim Kilfedder
who were with me throughout.

Nesta Wyn Ellis's book implied, firstly, that I had accepted a
free trip offered in a newspaper, and, secondly, that I had
subsequently reported falsely as a result. Neither allegation
was true. I took extreme care, as I say, only to comment on what
I saw with my own eyes, or to take evidence from eyewitnesses
who were trustworthy. For instance, the murder of a British tea-
planter, James Boyd, was reported to me by colleagues of his
who had actually been in his house on the night he was
abducted, and knew all the circumstances of his kidnapping,
and subsequent killing.

We saw some horrible things ourselves, particularly in and around Dacca, in the heart of East Pakistan. None of us will ever forget a jute factory some miles out of Dacca in jungle country. It has been the centre of a thriving community. The factory itself was quite large and the complex around it extensive. There were blocks of flats for all workers graded in size and architecture by the status of the workers who lived there. Executives, managers and foremen had the better homes; humble workers more basic ones. There was a football pitch, a school, a community centre and at least one shop.

Being out in the jungle it had been judged an unlikely target, and was not guarded by the Pakistani Army. Some three weeks before we went there, separatist soldiers had marched in unchallenged. All the workers were paraded onto the football field and shot dead, while their wives were forced to watch. Then the women were herded into the school hall and for the next two weeks were used as prostitutes by the soldiers. Finally, they were all murdered and the soldiers departed after killing the children with their swords.

We were taken there only two days after the soldiers had left. The bodies had gone but blood stains were everywhere. Small empty jewel boxes and a few ripped and blood-stained saris were strewn on the floor, all mingled with masses of dark matted hair which the grief-stricken women had ripped from their heads in an anguish of mourning. All the children were murdered in the Headmistress's small office and the scene of carnage was like no nightmare I have ever dreamed. Piles of brightly-coloured children's books were soaked in blood and all four walls were red with blood, spattered to a height of some four feet.

There had also been killing in many of the flats. We came away utterly sickened at what we had seen. I did send a despatch about this, but either it never got through, or was judged unsuitable for publication, for it never appeared.

The Delegation achieved at least one important success, not, of course, reported by Mrs Wyn Ellis. We had seen President Yahya Khan in West Pakistan, prior to going over to Dacca — a long journey around the southern tip of India, because at that time the Indian Government refused any over-flying of their country by Pakistani planes, so the flight from West Pakistan to East Pakistan (Bangladesh) took many hours instead of being a short hop. And we had to return later on, by the same route, so that we could see him again.

At the outset we said that we thought it was foolish that the foreign reporters had been sent out of the war area. Yahya Khan told us that he had trained at Sandhurst, and a basic part of the instruction was that, whenever a war was likely to break out, the first important step was to send out the women and children, and the foreign nationals. The press corps apparently came under the last heading, and out they went. This was extremely unwise, because, naturally, it led to biased reporting; and we urged Yahya Khan to let the press back in to see for themselves.

He was very doubtful, but finally he said that if we were of the same opinion when we had been across to East Pakistan and seen what was happening there, he would reconsider. When we did get back from Dacca, our first stop was the Presidential Palace. All we had seen convinced us even more that this was a story that needed to be told to the world. We therefore took the same line as before with Yahya Khan, urging him to drop his ban, and to invite the press back in. He was finally convinced, and sent for an Aide. We listened — without understanding a word — as he gave the man long and detailed instructions. Then as the Aide was leaving, Yahya Khan called him back and asked for one thing more.

He turned to us when the man had left, and explained that he had given instructions for the immediate withdrawal of the ban. His afterthought had been to call for a radio, so that we could all hear the English-language news on the hour. The radio was brought, switched on at the appropriate moment, and sure enough, the announcement was made that the world's press were again welcome in Pakistan.

This was, however, very late in the dispute — too late, as it turned out, to redress the balance of world opinion, which had already passed judgement on Pakistan. The Pakistanis were seen as being totally in the wrong, and had no alternative but to resign from the Commonwealth in the face of the opprobrium directed at them from so many quarters. Pakistani delegates vanished from the Commonwealth Parliamentary Association, and her High Commissioner in London became an Ambassador.

This situation is now, happily, reversed, and Pakistan is a member of the Commonwealth once more. It was a tragic interlude, though, and will remain as a shadow on the history of Pakistan's relationship both with the Commonwealth, and, by implication, with Great Britain.

There remains the running sore of Kashmir. In 1992 I visited the refugees in the camps of Muzaffarabad in the Pakistani sector of Kashmir, and heard from those who had suffered the brutality of the Indian Army occupying Srinagar and Indian Kashmir. There is great bitterness among Kashmiris that promises of self-determination made to them some 45 years ago by the UN have never been kept. There is resentment that Britain has not been more robust in pushing the issue.

The whole thing should have been settled in 1947 when the historic partition of India was brought about. Lord Louis Mountbatten, the last Viceroy, was in charge of the task of splitting Muslim Pakistan from Hindu India. There must have been many individual problems of territory and religion to solve, and the outcome took a terrible toll. Some 250,000 people died in the fighting following partition.

When it came to adjudicating over Kashmir, where a Hindu Kashmiri ruled over subjects who were mostly Muslim, Lord Mountbatten seems to have washed his hands of the problem. It has never been settled. The British government of the day, under Clement Attlee, probably thought the two resolutions on the United Nations agenda, which promised a plebiscite so that Kashmiris could vote on what future they wanted, would bring about a solution. Maybe they would have done; but in the event, those resolutions were never ratified. Instead, thousands flee the Indian-held section of Kashmir every year, and the stories of rape, maiming and killing by Indian troops are horrific.

After my visit to the Pakistani part of Kashmir in 1992, and my talks with the refugees in the border camps, I asked the Indian High Commissioner in London if I might go to Srinagar, on the Indian side, to see for myself what was going on there. He flatly refused my request.

CHAPTER EIGHTEEN

A Prime Minister Supplanted

A COLLEAGUE once told me something rather surprising about his driving. His normal aggressiveness at the wheel, which he attributes to years of coping with London traffic, transforms itself into sweetness and light on crossing the border into his constituency. All his family bore witness to this, he said. He would slow to about 5 mph at the sight of a pedestrian crossing, even if there was nobody anywhere near it. He would drive at a steady 29 mph, and approach every junction with swivelling eyes and instant readiness to give way, even when on a major road. He showed an alarming tendency to stop on seeing elderly citizens pausing at the roadside, just in case they wished to cross the road.

Discussing this later in the Smoking Room, all present agreed that, apart from the normal safety and legal considerations, utmost care is needed, politically, when behind a steering wheel — especially in one's constituency. Winging a pedestrian might well cost five or six votes, we felt. Then someone remarked thoughtfully that a striking a dog (even if it were unquestionably the dog's fault) would be infinitely worse. *That* could cost untold hundreds of votes. The British preference for animals over humans again! One cannot explain it, but one had better recognise and heed it. We are bound to consider the prejudices and preferences, as well as the needs, of our constituents, since they hold our future in their hands.

It is easy to annoy, and impossible to please, everyone. A certain action or reported speech will gain keen approval from one voter just as surely as it will infuriate another.

Canvassing with a Ward Chairman in one General Election campaign in Birmingham, I began with a cheerful smile and a

'Good morning, my name is Jill Knight and I have come about the General Election'.

Before I could finish the sentence the lady householder bristled. 'I know who you are', she said, 'and I'll make it clear straight away that I am certainly not voting for you.'

'Sorry to hear that', said I.

'It's your own fault. I've always voted for you before but I wrote and told you not to vote for the Seat Belts Bill. You wrote back and said you were going to, and I told you that, if you did, you would lose my vote. You *did* vote for it and you have lost my support. Like I said, it's your own fault.'

'Well', my colleague said mildly, 'the Seat Belts Bill has saved quite a lot of lives already.'

'That's just it!' she snapped. 'I'm a nurse, and because of you we haven't got any livers or hearts or corneas.'

This was unbelievable. 'You *can't* want people to die, just so that you can have their hearts and things, surely?' I quavered.

'I've told you: people *are* dying because they haven't got the hearts, and it's your fault. Good morning.' She slammed the door decisively. Astounded, we walked away, dazedly reflecting that you can't win 'em all.

Whether it be the European Community, capital punishment, abortion, daylight-saving schemes, euthanasia, trade union reform, privatisation or dog registration — some voters will be for, some against. How to reflect their wishes fairly at Westminster, then? The happy notion that one can do it the lazy way and be guided solely by opinion polls does not work, because the majority view may well have been reached more by gut reaction than calm thought, and is not necessarily the wisest conclusion. The only honest thing is to read all you can on the subject, listen to constituents as well as Ministers, weigh up the pros and cons and use your judgement. But an aspiring MP needs more than the judgement of Solomon. He (or she) must also have:

the tact of a diplomat;	the persistence of a debt-
the hide of an elephant;	collector; and
the energy of a break-dancer;	the patience of a saint.

A sense of humour is not essential, but oh brother — it helps!

Various other attributes will be called for from time to time, though it is not always easy to describe them. What, for instance, would be the tactic necessary in the following situation?

A tall, dark and undeniably handsome MP had been invited to present the prizes at a large comprehensive school for girls in his constituency. On such occasions the drill is always the same. First, the meeting with the school governors and senior members of staff in the Head's room over coffee and biscuits — or sherry (according to the time of day). Next, as the appointed hour grows near, one is gently shepherded into place and the procession enters the hall from the back, and files, in a dignified fashion, down the middle aisle. Massed ranks of parents, proud but nervous, are seated at the rear, and then pupils, seniors down to the youngest and those needing the eagle eye of authority on them, who are usually placed in the front row. Members of staff are strategically stationed along the route.

The platform party mounts the steps and unfalteringly takes up their correct chairs behind the platform table. Everything is always extremely well-organised and flows like an expertly-produced play. The Chairman of the Governors welcomes everyone, and the Head reads the Annual Report; the Honoured Guest is next invited to present the prizes, and does so, trying hard not to repeat exactly the same words of congratulation and encouragement to every recipient. He or she then makes a speech, the length of which, one is well aware, has probably been the subject of betting among the fourth years.

After that it is more or less plain sailing. Everyone visibly relaxes. The platform party retreats, this time with smiles directed right and left as it files out and into the Common Room, where, with a largish slice of the former audience, it is about to be fed the handiwork of caterers, or the cookery class, and plied with tea or coffee.

My colleague had reached this stage in the proceedings without mishap when a pretty little 16-year-old came up and offered him a plate of sausage rolls. He bent towards her in what he afterwards swore to me was an avuncular manner, and graciously selected one.

'Just a moment,' he said, 'didn't I present you with one of the prizes today?' The lassie blushed fetchingly. 'Yes', she whispered, smiling.

'Don't tell me, let me guess ... er, it was the geography prize!' Considering the sheer numbers he had just presented, the Member was justifiably pleased with himself for remembering.

'Yes,' she dimpled, with a toss of blonde curls, 'it was the geography prize.' But she did not move away. She stood there, sausage rolls apparently permanently on offer, while he munched on the one he had, and cast around for some other remark he might reasonably make.

'Er, you like geography?' he offered. 'Oh, yes', she nodded. 'I like geography *very* much.'

But *still* she did not move away. He was getting desperate. 'Um, what do you plan to do when you leave here?' he inquired, with thoughts of passing her on to the careers mistress, to whom he had been introduced earlier in the evening.

The young lady batted her eyelashes and patted her hair. 'Well', she cooed, 'as a matter of fact I have nothing arranged for this evening.'

I am not sure quite how he got out of that one; it is, thankfully, not a situation which would present itself to a female guest speaker.

There are far more women in the House of Commons than when I entered it. There is a very big difference in attitudes towards women, both inside and outside Westminster —

changes which have helped a lot. When I came in, a number of male MPs were openly resentful if women colleagues used the Smoking Room. There was a definite view that we should be tolerated rather than accepted, talked down to rather than treated as equals, and given certain jobs in certain categories only.

The very first committee I was asked to serve on was the Kitchen Committee, which organises the restaurants, the cafeterias and the bars used by MPs. I turned it down flat, stating firmly that I had not spent 10 years trying to get out of my kitchen, to go straight into the one in the House of Commons.

In 1966 the general public were still not entirely used to women taking up politics as a career. There were no women bank managers, and a woman could not be a member of the Stock Exchange, a General in the Army or the head of a nationalised industry. It was only eight years since the first woman had entered the House of Lords. Women were banned from membership of all the most prestigious London clubs, and if they were invited to lunch or dinner by a member, they were bundled in through an unobtrusive side entrance like a secret amour keeping a shady assignation. At the Carlton Club even the staircase up to the dining room was forbidden territory; one had to be wafted aloft unseen in an ancient elevator. Today all this has changed: the public not only expects to see women in positions of management, but applies pressure on institutions which do not put them there.

These changes came about for a number of reasons, including Parliamentary legislation, the work of the Equal Opportunities Commission (although this body has sometimes contrived to make itself look ridiculous), and the advent of Margaret Thatcher. As soon as a woman became Prime Minister it was clearly absurd that so many other positions of power and influence should be barred to women. The mighty Carlton Club yielded gracefully, welcoming her with acclamation as their first woman full member, and even the bastion of chauvinism, the forbidden staircase, fell — metaphorically speaking.

Margaret Thatcher became Leader of the Conservative Party in 1975 against all the odds, and went on to be one of the most remarkable Prime Ministers in British history. No unbiased observer can classify her achievements as less than phenomenal. Single-handed, she took on the might of the old-style Trade Unions — whose militancy and left-wing socialism all but ruined British industry in the 1960s and 1970s — and she won. She halted the tide of state ownership, by privatising the public utilities. She greatly increased home ownership through Council House sales, and brought back free enterprise. She fought, time and again, for a fairer deal for Britain in the European Community — and got it. Many leaders (and certainly Neil Kinnock) would have quailed at the prospect of waging a war on an enemy 8,000 miles away, and caved in to Argentina over the invasion of the Falklands. Mrs Thatcher stood firm; her courage and resolution carried the day and sent an unequivocal message to any other potential aggressor that Britain was not to be trifled with. Few realised what that campaign cost her. It is doubtful whether she slept for a single night during the entire campaign; and I saw personally the agony she went through on the day HMS Coventry was sunk.

The IRA tried to kill her, and very nearly succeeded, on that terrible night at the Conservative Party Conference in Brighton in 1984. Once again she displayed extraordinary coolness and courage.

No Prime Minister in modern times had been accorded the level of respect and admiration Mrs Thatcher attracted all over the globe. Perhaps her greatest achievement was to restore Britain's standing in the eyes of the world, which had indeed sunk to an all-time low before she took over.

However, the glowing adulation of the free world was very far from mirrored in Britain, where Mrs Thatcher became steadily more unpopular as time went on. There had been a campaign of character assassination against her by the media, and by the end of 1989 it had become fashionable to dislike and deride her. She was seen as arrogant, out of touch, and uncaring. Any stand-up comic was assured of an easy laugh with a reference to mad cow disease in Downing Street, or handbagging in Cabinet. Mere mention of her name on BBC's 'Question Time' would be greeted with boos and hisses. Worse, some of her own Cabinet colleagues whispered against her.

Undoubtedly she contributed to her own downfall. She no longer listened to those experienced colleagues who were her true friends. She flatly refused to take any notice of those Cabinet Ministers who warned that the 'Poll Tax', which was proposed to replace the old local 'Rates', was political dynamite. Once, an interview with Margaret would have her leaning forward, listening intently, asking probing questions and digesting carefully what had been said. Now, one had the unhappy feeling that she was tapping an impatient foot under the table, her mind on something else, longing for the interview to end.

She developed an extraordinary technique at parties and receptions at Number 10. She would stand at the door to greet her guests, who would take her extended hand. They would start to say something, only to find themselves pulled decisively across from right to left and straight into the reception room before they had articulated so much as a complete sentence. The impression given was certainly not that she was pleased to see you, but that you were a necessary irritation, and the sooner you got out of her way, the better.

It was not like that if you were invited to Chequers. There one felt still the old feeling that one was a friend and ally. But relatively few back-benchers were invited to Chequers, whereas most of them *did* experience the handshake that dismissed.

There were other things, too, that counted against her. One was a remark she made to a mass of television cameras and reporters, when her son's wife had a baby. 'We have become a grandmother', she said grandly. Why on earth didn't she keep to the simple 'I am now a grandmother'? Or if wishing not to exclude Denis, 'We have become grandparents'? The royal 'we' was widely commented upon and universally deplored.

After Ian Gow, Conservative Member for Eastbourne, was

murdered by the IRA in 1990, an apparently rock-solid Tory majority of 16,923 there was toppled: the Liberal Democrat candidate got in with a majority of 4,550 votes at the by-election on 18 October. On 8 November of the same year there was a by-election in the the highly marginal seat of Bradford, which Labour had held previously by 1,633. The new Labour candidate won by a comfortable 9,514 votes.

A growing number of Conservative MPs began to believe uneasily that the Conservatives could not win the next General Election under Margaret Thatcher. An even larger group of colleagues, bitter either because they had never been made Ministers by Mrs Thatcher or because they had been sacked from their Ministerial appointments by her, joined the first group in a bid to oust her. Yet she still had a solid core of support in the Parliamentary Party. No leadership election would have taken place in the Autumn of 1990 if it had not been for a truly astounding speech by Sir Geoffrey Howe on 13 November, which blew the whole situation wide open. He had resigned as Leader of the House and Deputy Prime Minister on 30 October and now claimed his right to make a personal statement as to the reasons for his resignation. Everyone crowded into the Chamber to listen. Immediately after Parliamentary Questions were over, this mild and bumbling man rose to his feet from what was, for him, a most unaccustomed place on the Back Benches below the gangway.

Incredibly, for 20 minutes he directed a tirade of the most vicious and explicit abuse at his former colleague, with a ferocity and venom never before heard in a speech in the House by a Conservative *about* a Conservative. Whatever we had expected, it was not this. Members were stunned. Some felt physically sick as Geoffrey continued to twist the knife in the wound, and the Labour Party's grins grew wider. The Prime Minister herself sat pale and stony-faced on the Front Bench.

It was patently obvious that a leadership election was now inevitable, and on the next day Michael Heseltine announced his challenge to Margaret Thatcher. I had long regretted Michael's absence from the Front Bench. Of course, he had been impulsive in wielding the Mace four years earlier,[1] and in walking out of Cabinet over the Westland affair, thus resigning from office. But before that he had done a marvellous job as Secretary of State for the Environment, particularly in Liverpool where he was greatly admired and respected. He had charisma, and the rank-and-file Conservative audiences adored him. Furthermore, since his resignation he had spent the extra time this had given him going round the country tirelessly speaking for the Party, and many colleagues had reason to feel grateful to him. He never refused to speak at any meeting, big or small, nor help in any by-election. He was never for one moment disloyal to the Conservative Party, nor to Mrs Thatcher herself.

However, at that time my first loyalty was to Mrs Thatcher. While I acknowledged that she had faults, these seemed to me pygmies beside her achievements, and I voted for her in the first ballot on 20 November. The result was 204 votes for Margaret Thatcher and 152 for Michael Heseltine, with 16 void or spoilt papers. This majority did not satisfy the rules of the Conservative Party for the election of a Party leader, and it was therefore necessary to hold a second ballot. This the Chairman of the 1922 Committee announced would take place on the following Tuesday, with nominations closing on 22 November.

At the time of the first ballot, Margaret Thatcher herself was in Paris, taking part in the Conference on Security and Co-operation in Europe, and she voted by proxy. As soon as the result of the first ballot was known, the Chief Whip telephoned it to her. Without waiting to consult, or reflect, she announced immediately to the waiting television cameras that she would fight again in the second ballot. Michael Heseltine let it be known that he too would contest that ballot, and his nomination was handed in on the morning of 21 November.

---

[1] When the Mace is on its stand on the desk in front of the Speaker, the House is in session. If anyone picks it up or even places a hand on it, the sitting is automatically suspended.

Mrs Thatcher, once back from Paris, found that her Cabinet was very much less than solid in her support. All that day advice poured in from different sections of the Party, and it was conflicting. As the hours went by it became clear that her victory over Michael Heseltine was very far from assured. Defeat and humiliation were a distinct possibility. On the following morning, at 9:38 a.m., after what surely must have been a sleepless night, she announced her decision not to stand in the second ballot; she would resign as soon as a new Leader was elected. By the time nominations closed at noon on that same day there were three candidates — Michael Heseltine, John Major and Douglas Hurd.

Only four hours later, the Labour Leader Neil Kinnock opened the debate on a No Confidence motion tabled by the Opposition. Margaret Thatcher replied for the Government with the finest speech of her career. She utterly destroyed Neil Kinnock's arguments; her speech was witty, brave, and moving, too. The No Confidence motion was defeated, but her triumph was as much personal as political. More than one Honourable Member was in tears as she spoke, and I heard someone murmur: 'What have we done?'.

From the beginning to the end of the Leadership Crisis I tried hard to sound out opinion in my Constituency. I was involved, through my membership of the Executive of the 1922 Committee, in consultations with many sections of the Party, and with the House of Lords. But in the final analysis, one must make up one's own mind — and this is no bad thing, because Parliamentary colleagues really do know each other better than outsiders can. I had been severely berated 15 years earlier by a number of my constituents because I supported Mrs Thatcher in her leadership challenge against Mr Heath. Subsequent events certainly proved the correctness of *that* judgement, so I faced this decision reasonably confidently. I voted for Michael Heseltine for reasons I have earlier indicated. The result of the ballot on 27 November was 185 votes for John Major, 131 for Michael Heseltine and 56 for Douglas Hurd. There were no spoiled papers. Technically, John Major's majority was not

quite enough to satisfy the Conservative Party's rules for a
leadership election, and for a ghastly 15 minutes we thought
there would have to be a third ballot. However, immediately
following the declaration, both Michael Heseltine and Douglas
Hurd announced that they intended to withdraw, and would be
asking their supporters to vote for John Major. We had a new
Prime Minister, and, as one would expect, the Party immediately
rallied behind him.

At that time, few knew what John Major was made of. A
quiet and unassuming man, firm but with charm, his tenures as
Chancellor of the Exchequer and Foreign Secretary were both
too short to have enabled him to make much of an impact on
the public. He certainly was to have a baptism of fire. Economic
difficulties at home were daunting; and within a few weeks he
found himself Prime Minister of a country at war. Saddam
Hussain, the dictator of Iraq, had marched into Kuwait, and our
troops were involved as part of the United Nations force.

John Major was no Margaret Thatcher; but then, a seriously
large section of the public had indicated that they wanted a
different kind of Prime Minister, and John was certainly that.

He was later to prove just as courageous as his predecessor,
though much more unlucky in the difficulties he had to face.
Yet his transparent honesty of purpose and determination to do
what he saw as best for Britain began steadily to win him
admiration and support.

CHAPTER NINETEEN
The Hazards of Winning

JOHN MAJOR won the General Election in June 1992 against all the odds. No-one believed the Conservatives would win. The opinion polls were a consistent disaster for the Conservative Party, and Labour were utterly confident of victory.

It was a miserable hustings. In the whole three weeks of the campaign, it only stopped raining once. My loyal helpers slogged it out with me on the doorsteps, umbrellas dripping disconsolately, quite unequal to the task of keeping us dry. We must have looked more like a party of drowned rats than a confident canvass team, but we kept doggedly on.

On the very worst day, towards the evening, a report on BBC TV declared the Labour Party 26 points ahead in the polls — with only a week to go.

At this point, with victory seemingly in the bag, the Labour Party leaders made a serious error of judgement. They staged a rally in Sheffield, which turned into a TV spectacular. They assumed to themselves Cabinet posts, giving 'the new Prime Minister', Neil Kinnock, a presidential-style greeting. It was all too much. It jolted the voter into serious contemplation and, perhaps for the first time in the campaign, to recognition of how woefully inadequate were the political arguments and policies Labour spokesmen were peddling.

In the event, the Conservative Party did take a mauling — 44 seats lost, including three in Birmingham. The Conservatives nonetheless retained a majority of 21 seats over all other parties, and we took our places again on the right of the Speaker in the Chamber, as the governing party always does. Betty Boothroyd was elected as Speaker for the new Parliament, the first lady to hold the post, and she has proved herself an able and popular occupant of that most difficult of chairs.

The honeymoon for John Major's new government did not last long. The first really big confrontation came in October after the summer recess. Michael Heseltine, now President of the Board of Trade, announced that 31 coal mines were to be closed, with the loss of 30,000 jobs.

Not surprisingly, all hell broke loose. The miners, who had been reviled at the time of the Scargill strikes, were abruptly cast in a Mom-and-apple-pie role. The suddenness of the announcement, coupled with public apprehension at the prospect of so many unemployed miners, induced a strong and furious response. How could the Government be so callous? It was not a bit of use recalling that the Labour Party when in office had closed well over double the number of pits now doomed by the Conservatives, with a loss of not 30,000, but 186,000 jobs. It cut no ice that the miners were to be offered redundancy money (on average £23,000 per miner), and retraining. It made no difference that the demand for coal had fallen; that too many pits were neither making a profit nor had any prospect of so doing. The fury of the electorate was expressed to every MP, by letter, telephone, and in person at MPs' advice bureaux.

Michael Heseltine himself appeared astounded at the force of the attack on him. He had lived for months with the knowledge that an uneconomic industry could not forever be propped up by the taxpayer. But the taxpayers themselves had other ideas. They, and the Labour Party, felt there had to be another way: somehow surely, the pits could be saved.

Governments, however, are like King Canute. There are many things over which they have no control. It may be that a Labour Government, had we had one then, would have subsidised loss-making pits indefinitely, funding this via extra taxation. Or perhaps not — they refused to do that when they were in power. Nothing forces a political party to face reality so much as holding the reins of government. It was only the luxury of being in opposition which fuelled their attacking fire in that quarrelsome Autumn of 1992.

Some Conservative MPs had pits in their constituencies, too.

They fought against the closures with just as much vigour as did Labour MPs, and no-one was happy at Mr Heseltine's proposals. The row rumbled on for months. There was a stay of execution for some mines; every possible alternative to closure was examined, but the unpalatable truth finally had to be faced. Most of the pits were closed in the end, as Michael Heseltine had said they would be, though some 30 were bought by groups of enterprising miners determined to try and make a go of it.

In spite of the payment of redundancy money and stalwart efforts to bring new industries to the mining areas, the result was often hardship and unemployment in the pit communities. The deepening recession thwarted some plans to open small businesses with the cash payouts. Yet it is difficult to see what else could have been done. It is sad, but also ironic — I well recall being taught as a child that one day, when a better age dawned, we would not send men thousands of feet below ground to work in a dark and dangerous place where gas could blow them up, tunnel collapses could kill them, and coal dust would shorten their breath, and their lives. Never for a moment had I envisaged that the ending of all this would be greeted with such fury and resentment.

Some 10 or 15 years prior to these events, it had been decided (quite rightly) that Members of Parliament knew too little about industry. Among the Parliamentary roll-call are plenty of solicitors, barristers, and others with backgrounds in teaching, lecturing, accountancy and so on. Businessmen, however, usually deduce (correctly) that financial rewards are better, hours are shorter and leisure less interrupted, outside the House. As a result, MPs with experience in business are thin on the Westminster ground.

Because it was felt this ignorance of business procedure should be addressed, the Industry and Parliament Trust was set up. Under its auspices, a long list of industries was compiled, each standing ready to take on an MP as visitor, student and observer. The MPs would thus learn about how the various industries conducted their business; and so it has come about. The only snag is that an MP has to assign 25 days in a year, to undertake this study. In our busy lives, this is a great deal of time. And in the Parliament which followed the 1992 Election, it had become far more difficult — particularly when the Labour Party, by the end of 1993, had withdrawn all pairing arrangements.

Nonetheless, it seemed important to take on this challenge. By a piece of good fortune for which I have never ceased to be immensely grateful, I was assigned to Royal Doulton. My studies with them started in earnest in 1993. Off I went to Stoke-on-Trent, to learn how china is made. They taught me what bone china is, and why it is both delicate and strong; then about the stringent and very expensive chemical tests that have to be made to satisfy the American market, because of what is actually a miniscule use of lead in the manufacturing process. They moved on to show me the entrancing business of creating a design; they demonstrated the processes of decoration of the objects they produce — by hand-painting, and using transfers. I watched the modelling of animals, Toby jugs, character jugs, pretty ladies, and nursery-story figures. Next I was taught all about crystal, and learned to appreciate the stunning beauty of expert glass-cutting. Then to marketing — quite a different field, done in a dozen ways, to advertise and sell the product nationally and internationally.

It was a door opened onto a new world of experience for me, and no firm could have been more patient or kind, in dealing with a novice outsider, than was Royal Doulton. It has left me with a knowledge and a deep appreciation of fine china, and reinforced my belief in the quality of British expertise and enterprise. More than that, when visiting cities all over the world, I now find myself veering automatically towards the china departments of the large stores, to check if they are stocking Royal Doulton, and if so, which patterns sell best.

There are many quirks to that. The heavily decorated Imari

design, all scarlet and blue and 22-carat gold, is most popular of all among gypsies. This is extremely expensive china, collected partly as an investment and partly as a status symbol. Romany caravans are full of it. Amazing! And who would have guessed that it is almost impossible to sell china decorated with birds, in mining areas? Years ago, caged birds (canaries mostly) were taken down the pits because they could detect gas and would die from it before any human would. They were used as natural early-warning systems, and are still considered very unlucky wherever mining went on.

In June 1994, Pearson, the former parent company of Royal Doulton, asked me to approach Madam Speaker with an offer of a special set of china for the Speaker's House. The dinner service would be decorated with a design by the noted Victorian architect and designer, Augustus Welby Pugin. He designed the interior for the new Houses of Parliament, after the old Palace of Westminster was destroyed by fire in 1834. Also, inside the new building, which was built in the Gothic style by the father and son architects Charles and Edward Barry, there is furniture and china designed by Pugin.

The Rt Hon Betty Boothroyd (having prudently checked with me to ensure that it was dishwasher safe) accepted, and I took a small delegation from Pearson and Doulton to make the presentation. This generous gift of 40 place-settings coincided with a major exhibition in the Victoria and Albert Museum, which commemorated Pugin's designs and achievements.

The range of major firms which have welcomed and taught their MP attachments under the Industry and Parliament Trust is immensely wide. ICI, Reed International, Unilever, Blue Circle Cement, British Rail, Post Offices, Marks and Spencer, British Gas, Esso and Mars are just a few of them. Members have learned about how airlines work, how hotels function, about banking, farming and the manufacture of scores of things from trucks and homes to pills and potions. They have been on oil rigs, down in submarines, and have gone deep into Britain's countryside, while studying agriculture.

If all of my colleagues learned as much on their courses as I

did on mine, the House must certainly be a more knowledge-
able place than before the Industry and Parliament Trust came
into being. But before I finished my study period with Royal
Doulton, there was big trouble elsewhere.

CHAPTER TWENTY
Handing On the Torch

THE Summer of 1993 was a bad-tempered affair at Westminster. The European Communities (Amendment) Bill, which aimed at implementing the Maastricht Treaty, was grinding through the House. There were some 50 Tory rebels, all of whom, to a greater or lesser degree, were opposed to Britain being a member of the Community at all. This was in spite of the fact that the decision to be so had been taken by a national referendum years previously, and the Manifesto on which all Conservative candidates fought the 1992 election included specific support for the Maastricht Treaty, signed in December 1991.

Not that all of us who steadily voted in the Government lobbies, throughout the months from November 1992 to July 1993, were starry-eyed about all aspects of our membership of the European Community. There was much concern at examples of EC rulings reaching out to ban practices which had been carried out perfectly safely in Britain for years. One butcher's shop was harried out of existence by their local Environmental Health Officers (later justly named the Food Police), who insisted that the shop would need a new door, and completely new floor and wall tiles. It mattered not to them that the little business had been going along happily and hygienically since 1929; nor that the customers complained, in a body, at their ruling. It was EC regulations — said the officials. The builders' costs were more than the butcher could pay; there was nowhere another door could be put in anyway, and the business was forced to close down.

Later it became apparent that the Environmental Health Officers were being over-zealous, and there were several more instances of the same kind. Often there were loopholes which could have been used to bypass regulations, but these were ignored. Britain, alone of all the Community countries, follows every last dot and comma of an EC ruling obediently, and the result has often sparked resistance to our membership in home circles, which was not there before.

Throughout this period the anecdotal evidence of the 'intolerable interference from Brussels' was sometimes alarming and sometimes funny. Fishermen were to be forced to wear hair-nets; double-decker buses were to be banned; gin bottles would have to be round, not square; curved cucumbers, prawn crisps and the sale of home-made jam would all be outlawed. All these rumours circulated, and all were untrue. They did, however, contribute to public concern, which filtered through unerringly to MPs, in their constituency mail, and their advice bureaux.

It is entirely right that Britain's sovereignty and ability to manage her own affairs must be safeguarded. But under the terms of the Maastricht Treaty Britain took a step *back* from too-close involvement with EC rulings. John Major ensured, over the days and nights of discussion and argument, that the Community could only take action if an objective could not be better achieved at the national level (the so-called 'subsidiarity clause'). He succeeded in deleting 'Federalism' as an aim of the EC. He got agreement, in a legally-binding protocol, that Britain, and Britain alone, should decide whether she would subscribe to a single currency, and if so, when. He got the 'Social Chapter' dropped from the draft Treaty — with the other member-states agreeing to accept a 'Social Charter' binding on them but not on us. This last achievement was of great importance to British industry, and indeed to all of us who had experienced the disaster of militant union power in Britain.

John Major has never had the praise he deserved for his skill in the Maastricht negotiations. Officials present were deeply impressed at the way he mastered an extremely complicated brief, and quietly, but with force and logic, argued Britain's corner. At the negotiating table, he had to be quite alone, unable to consult, and yet be ready to counter fast manoeuvres with facts and figures. He did it brilliantly.

However, the Tory rebels at Westminster were spoiling for a fight, and, with the help of the Opposition, they got one. The Labour Party voted, not always from conviction, nor in keeping with their past speeches, but with the scent of blood in their nostrils. They saw a chance to defeat the Government and cause a General Election.

There was one issue on which the Labour Party were totally consistent — whether Britain should go along with the Euro diktat, embedded in the Social Charter, on the matter of enforcing a compulsory minimum wage for all in work. Labour's argument for this seems to me fatally flawed. For everyone, idle or industrious, clever or dull, competent or incompetent, to be able to claim a certain sum makes no economic sense. An employee is worth what he is worth to his employer. The employer has to market a product which people will buy, at a price they can afford. No law can force a shopper to purchase, and if the law forces an employer to pay his employee more than that person is worth, one of two things will happen. Either the price of the article will be too high and the factory will go out of business, or the employer will choose not to employ the incompetent at all. Either way, an enforced minimum wage will lead to unemployment.

All this was surely basic Conservative belief, and indeed up until the Maastricht Treaty there had never been disagreement among our ranks that the Social Charter was anathema. Now the clause on our opt-out offered the rebels a chance of success, in beating the Government on Maastricht; and to their eternal discredit, some of them took it.

The crunch came on 22 July 1993. Enough of the Conservative anti-marketeers voted with Labour, against the Government's opting out of the Social Charter, for us to lose the vote by one. John Major immediately announced that there would be a Motion of Confidence in the Government laid in the House on the following day. The rebels knew they were beaten, for if they voted against the Government on *that*, a General Election would follow, in which it was clear (given the widespread unpopularity of the Government and the way by-elections were going) that many would lose their seats. We all lived to fight another day, and the 'Maastricht Bill' went through.

I have written earlier of the four Bills I introduced which became law. In the Spring of 1994 I introduced another Private Member's Bill, under the 'Ten Minute Rule'. Years before, when fighting David Steel's Abortion Bill of 1966, I put down and sought to debate an amendment to ensure that aborted babies should not be used for scientific experiments. The Speaker of the day rebuked me, saying that my amendment was wrong, emotive, and totally unnecessary. The little bodies would always be treated with respect; they would never be chopped around or utilised by scientists.

By 1994 all this had changed. Such practices had become accepted and commonplace. Parliament had been told four years earlier that human embryo experiments were vital for preventing, or even curing, diseases. They would help discover why some children were born deformed. These claims have not so far been substantiated, but they were believed. The Human Fertilisation and Embryology Authority was set up by the Government, and charged with the task of monitoring scientific experimentation in this field, and granting licences for it.

Now there came the news that scientists were within reach of being able to use the eggs from aborted girl babies to fertilise infertile women. The HFEA set up a consultation process, but this seemed clearly to be aimed at getting agreement for it. Everyone was told soothingly that although the idea might seem rather offensive at first, people would 'soon get used to it'. Scientists disparagingly described the moral outrage of many at the suggested practice, as 'the yuk factor'. It was obvious that a softening-up process was going on, and that if nothing was done, this immoral and repugnant procedure would slip into normal practice.

Therefore, on 22 February 1994, I introduced my Ten-Minute Rule Bill to prohibit the use of eggs from aborted foetuses for fertilisation purposes. Colleagues from all parties and all parts of Britain hurried to offer their sponsorship of my measure. There was no opposing speaker, and my Bill was over the first hurdle. However, it would only proceed if it could be attached to a major Bill going through the House. Somewhat to my surprise, I found that it would be perfectly in order for me to turn it into a new clause to the Criminal Justice and Public Order Bill.

Mrs Virginia Bottomley, the then Secretary of State for Health, though supporting the Human Fertilisation and Embryology Authority in general, listened to my arguments with immense care, and came to agree. She subsequently gave me verbal backing, as well as access to advice from Government drafters, to ensure that my new clause was watertight.

I moved the clause late in the evening of 12 April 1994. The timing was not my choice — one simply has to speak on clauses in the order in which they come. Some 300 colleagues trooped into the division lobby to support me, but although there were three speeches against me in the debate, not even two tellers could be found to carry through a vote against. So the Division was called off, and the new clause was approved without a vote.

The general public loved me: the scientists hated me. Why was I seeking to prohibit this treatment before the consultation with the Human Fertilisation and Embryology Authority was completed?

Why? Partly because the consultation process was suspect. Even MPs were not sent the document setting out the options, until I complained. When meetings were held in different parts of the country, reports filtering back indicated that they were not conducted fairly. From what I heard, the meetings were deliberately 'packed' with supporters, and those wishing to speak against were dealt with summarily. The chairman of one meeting declared openly that no notice would be taken of those against the proposal.

Why move the clause now, it was asked, when it would probably be years before scientists were actually able to make a woman pregnant in this way? My answer to this was that it seemed sensible to stop money and time being poured into research to perfect a process which would never be allowed to be used.

Why prevent a woman from using her own aborted child's eggs? This was also raised as a serious question, yet it seemed to me the silliest proposition of all. If a woman had become pregnant in the first place, she must have had either her own eggs, or access to donated ones. What woman would wish to carry her dead child's baby — and so bear her own grandchild?

I made it plain that the Bill (and thus the new clause) did not stop research, simply the use of foetal eggs for the specific purpose of enabling fertilisation. There are millions of women in Britain alone who are of child-bearing age, and able to donate eggs to the women who long for children. One has every sympathy for women faced with infertility; but surely it would be better to embark upon a campaign to persuade women to donate their eggs, just as blood donors have been persuaded to give their blood?

The row rumbled on. I received countless letters of support — and four against me.

Baroness Warnock sought to destroy the effect of the clause when it reached the House of Lords, via an amendment. She then withdrew hers, in favour of a similarly intentioned amendment by Lord Walton of Detchant. The clause seemed destined to be debated in the night hours, for it was after midnight on 17 June 1994 that it was reached. Nevertheless, a number of peers and peeresses spoke in favour of the clause and against the amendment, and Lord Walton withdrew it, though he threatened to fight again at Report Stage. In fact, he did not do so. The clause passed into law with the Act to which it was attached. I now had my fifth Private Member's Bill safely on the Statute Book.

John Major's Government had achieved a great deal, but those achievements were obliterated from the public's notice by a whole series of unsavoury incidents, seized on avidly and trumpeted loudly by a media apparently determined to ensure trouble for the Government. Not that some Conservative MPs did not contribute. There were minor and major scandals, often of a sexual nature, involving back-bench MPs and even Ministers. There were damaging leaks from official documents. Two Tory Members were involved in a 'cash for questions' scandal, and there were allegations of illegal sales of arms. There were misjudgements, and there were unending squabbles over Europe.

All this totally obscured Government successes. The British economy, entirely due to tough and unpopular measures taken by Government, was in better shape than every other country in Europe, as the OECD has confirmed. Our unemployment figures were falling in a way other countries openly envied. But the all-important 'feel-good' factor was not materialising. The housing market was stagnant. Many people saw the value of the homes they had bought so proudly sink well below the amount they had borrowed to pay for those homes. The Health Service had never been so successful, with far more people treated and cured than ever before, but the newspapers concentrated on the few failures and never mentioned the millions of successes. Law and order worried the electorate, most of whom appeared to blame every crime on the Government in spite of numerous measures, from greatly increased help for the police to the mammoth 1994 Criminal Justice and Public Order Bill, which contained some very tough provisions indeed. And so it went on. Support for the Conservatives steadily eroded. By-elections were lost, Council seats fell, and in the local elections in May 1995 some 2,000 Tory Councillors were defeated.

The mood in the Parliamentary Party was bad. Divisions over Europe and tax policy, allied to a growing fear of losing their seats at the next General Election, led to mutinous rumblings and grumblings about the Leadership. All sorts of rumours were circulated by the Press. One such claimed that the Prime Minister had been summoned to appear before the Executive of the 1922 Committee and ordered to carry out a catalogue of tax and other changes. It was totally untrue. Finally, in a dramatic bid to regain party unity and reassert his authority, John Major astounded the Party and the country by announcing his resignation as leader, and his candidature in the Leadership election which inevitably would swiftly follow. On the sunny lawn of No. 10 Downing Street on 22 June 1995 he called on his detractors to 'put up or shut up'.

Fifteen minutes before he told the Press, he had informed the Executive of the 1922 Committee of his decision at a special meeting in his room at the House of Commons. I remember remarking to a colleague as, totally stunned, we filed out: 'I suppose that is what is meant by lancing the boil.'

John Major's judgement in calling that leadership election was absolutely right. Had he not done so, a cauldron of resentment would have bubbled away through July, August and September, up to the all-important Party Conference season in October. Even that would not have been the end, for the Parliamentary Party holds its leadership elections in November. It was too long for the doubts and uncertainties to last.

The next 12 days were days of high drama. The Secretary of State for Wales, John Redwood, resigned and announced his candidature for the Leadership. Westminster was in a ferment, though I do not believe that John Major himself was troubled in the least. If he won, he won; if he didn't, he would work with the new Leader for a Conservative victory at the next General Election.

In the event, with 329 Conservatives eligible to vote, John Major won 218 votes, while John Redwood trailed badly with 89. The issue was settled. Although technically it would be possible to challenge again in November, we all knew it would not happen. With such a decisive victory, which was bigger than Margaret Thatcher ever managed, and more than double the majority achieved by Tony Blair in Labour's Leadership contest, there would be no question of another Leadership battle in the Conservative Party in 1995, and hopefully not before the next General Election.

Though I shall not be a candidate at that Election, I will never leave the field of political endeavour, believing as profoundly as I do that Conservative principles and Conservative policies serve our dear country best.